T0196951

PREVIOUS BOOKS

Healing by Contacting Your Cells.
Journal Excerpts From the Ring of Fire.
What Can You Do To Help Our World?
2013 And Beyond.
2013 And Beyond Part II.
2014 World Journals.
2015 World Healing.

2015 WORLD HEALING II

Barbara Wolf & Margaret Anderson

authorHOUSE®

AuthorHouse™
1663 Liberty Drive
Bloomington, IN 47403
www.authorhouse.com
Phone: 1 (800) 839-8640

Published by AuthorHouse   12/15/2015

ISBN: 978-1-5049-6815-7 (sc)
ISBN: 978-1-5049-6813-3 (hc)
ISBN: 978-1-5049-6814-0 (e)

Library of Congress Control Number: 2015920614

Print information available on the last page.

This book is dedicated to Barbara's husband
Jack and to the rest of the world.

ACKNOWLEDGEMENTS

Hideo Nakazawa and Masami Saionji, Japan
Carmen Balhestero, Brazil
Master Goi and Saint Germain
Chief Golden Light Eagle, Lakota Nation
Grandmother SilverStar, Cherokee/Lakota Nation
Ronna Herman and Archangel Michael
James Tyberonn and Archangel Metatron
Fred Sterling and Kirael
Patricia Cota-Robles
Pele and Fuji
David J. Adams, Australia
Uqualla, Havasupai Tribe, Grand Canyon
Victoria Lee, Mount Shasta
Prageet and Julieanne Conard, Stargate
Mike and Ruth Ssembiro, Uganda
Pope Francis, Vatican City
Emma Kunz, visionary artist healer
Paul Winter, musician
Anton Mizerak and Laura Berryhill, musicians
Bearcloud, artist
Lyman Whitaker, sculptor
Annette Price, On the Wings of a Horse
John Ninfo, Wild Wings, Ganondagan
G. Peter Jemison, Ganondagan

Barbara Wolf & Margaret Anderson

Ashfaq Ishaq, International Child Art Foundation
Eric Salvisberg and Do Spiegel, Europe
Judy Moss, healer, researcher, friend
Nikola Tesla, inventor

FOREWORD

We firmly believe in what we believe, and we
realize you may not agree with everything we believe.
Probably we would not agree with everything you
agree with. But let us put aside our differences and
let us be friends.

It's the world that matters. Mother Earth needs help
and we are trying to give it to her. That is all that is
expected.

CONTENTS

Acknowledgements.. vii

Foreword ix

Introduction.. xiii

Chapter 1   World Children's Festival..1

Chapter 2   Sedona Journey..6

Chapter 3   Sedona Journey...18

Chapter 4   Mount Shasta Journey 27

Chapter 5   Mount Shasta Journey 36

Chapter 6   Niagara Falls..47

Chapter 7   Niagara Falls..57

Chapter 8   Pope Francis Comes To U.S.A. 62

Chapter 9   Buffalo, Horses, Birds
             Buffalo...75

Chapter 10 Native American Ganondagan...89

Chapter 11 To Mother Earth, With Love 97

Glossary 109

Vortex Symbols And Earthstar Calendar 113

INTRODUCTION

We think our world will be peaceful and happy when people are peaceful and happy with each other. Our book begins with children competing peacefully in music, dance and art at a World Children's Festival. This teaches non-violence which will remain with them.

We write about going to Sedona, one of the most peaceful areas of the North American continent. The scenery of red mountains and forests is gorgeous and creates a desire to stay forever. Then we go to towering Mount Shasta whose energy is positive, spectacular. Like Sedona, one wants to live there forever.

Niagara Falls is another powerful place, and riding the Maid of the Mist boat within the falls itself is a wonderful experience. We stand with strangers at the railing, laughing, gasping, as water cascades over us. And then we tell you about seeing the new Vatican Pope whose friendly attitude brings shouts of joy by thousands of strangers as he rides by.

We take a break from being with our human family and spend a bit of time enjoying the nature world of the buffalo, horses, birds. This is followed by visiting Ganondagan, a peaceful Native American community.

CHAPTER 1

WORLD CHILDREN'S FESTIVAL

From Barbara:

July 1, just before 6 a.m., Margaret and I board an Amtrak train to take us to New York City to board another train for Washington D.C.

Why are we going to Washington D.C.? We will be attending a WCF, a World Children's Festival where children globally compete with each other in music and dance and art. They will be competing peacefully and not with violence on their minds. They will be learning how to accept strangers and foreigners without reacting negatively, and when they finish their schooling, their former peaceful competitive experience can help them remain peaceful.

Our friend Mike Ssembiro of Uganda has told us he took children to the last competition and they won first prize. He will again be taking a group of children to compete this year and we have told him we will attend and support these children.

Will the Ugandans win first prize again? If they do, they do. If not, never mind. We will go to Washington anyway to watch them perform.

But now, less than a week before Mike and the children are to fly from Africa to Washington D.C., they do not have visas for entering the U.S.A.

WHAT!

We learn that on June 8, visa regulations to come to the U.S.A. have changed for anyone living elsewhere in the world. And so, the process of issuing visas has been stalled.

HOW CAN THIS BE????????

I phone the White House and speak with an excellent 'listener' who patiently tells me that the White House can do nothing. Only the State Department can do something.

And so I phone the State Department one time, two times, three times, then four times before I can actually speak to someone who will listen to me about the visa problem and the children ready to compete in Washington D.C.

I am told that only the specific U.S. Embassy issuing the Ugandan visas can help.

Well........... I am doubtful that is the only place that can help, but............. what can one do?

I phone Mike and his wife in Uganda and urge them to connect with someone in the Ugandan President's office who can phone the U.S. Embassy to urge a moving along of the visas. I know Mike and his wife have close contact with the President's office.

The next day, when I again phone them, I learn that some of the children have received their visas. Others, including Mike, will receive them on June 30. That is the day their plane will be leaving for the U.S.A.!

Well, one can only keep one's fingers crossed that the visas are issued in time.

And yes, later, when I reach Washington, I learn that all have received visas, including Mike.

As for Margaret and me, when we begin our journey by train, we go first to New York City in order to transfer to a Washington D.C. train. But........ WHAT IS THIS? Our train to New York arrives just under two hours late, and our train for Washington D.C. is ready to leave within fifteen minutes.

We grab a 'red cap' baggage handler to help race us to the train. First, he takes us to an ascending escalator where he squats, and with a key, he stops the upward movement of the escalator and changes it to descend!

We race down it and then race along corridors to reach the train, which, for some unknown reason, is empty. It is not going anywhere.

And so the 'red cap' races us upstairs to service counters where many are waiting in line to be served. The 'red cap' bypasses all of them to reach a service counter specifically used by 'red caps' to get prompt service.

Our tickets are changed so we will leave for Washington just after 3 p.m., and now the 'red cap' takes us to this train, which is empty. We sit in it and wait about a half hour before others begin boarding.

When all are aboard and the train begins moving slowly along underground tracks, we wait patiently for 'day light'. And yes, when it comes, we love the sun shining above us. We know there has been much rain down here and we would prefer that none falls while we are here.

When we come to our first stop, Newark Station, some passengers get off and others get on, which is normal. But, we are puzzled when a conductor walking along the train aisle announces we are on our way to Richmond via Philadelphia.

ARE WE ARE ON THE WRONG TRAIN?????

My memory is that we go nearly directly from New York City to Washington and certainly not to Philadelphia and Richmond. He has not even mentioned we are going to Washington.

We flag down another conductor who says yes, we will eventually reach Washington. I do not ask, but I wonder why we are first going to the south of Washington and then north to reach it.

Well, I do not have a road map, and so one has to depend on the train reaching Washington no matter how strange is the route.

And yes, after we do go south, we are told we will soon reach Washington, and that our engine has to be changed. WHY?????

We do not ask why, but one begins to think that traveling by a means other than by train would bring less anxiety.

FINALLY though, we reach our destination, Union Station, and we pick up our bags, leave the train and walk to a sidewalk that has access to taxis. Nearly twelve hours of riding trains is enough for one day.

Our hotel, the Washington Court Hotel, suggested by Amtrak when we bought our tickets, is close to the train station and we are immediately impressed with the place. It looks new; is spacious, and our room on the eighth floor looks like no one had ever used it. We have dinner in the downstairs dining room overlooking the spacious lobby.

July 1:

I peek out the window. Is it raining? No. GOOD.

We eat a quick breakfast and then we are on our way to the Ellipse where the children's competition will be held. This is a very big grassy area behind the White House. Apparently, this Ellipse was originally water before it was filled in. Just now, because Washington has had much rain, the grass at the Ellipse is soggy. I note that the grass is long and should have been cut before the children's festival. Maybe it was too wet to be cut before the festival. One has to watch one's step while walking! Here and there are soggy patches that become somewhat deep. A misstep could bring water into the shoes!

In any case, our attention is on the outdoor covered stage that is wooden and circular with a number of chairs facing it. The children will be competing here, and we choose chairs in the first row. By coincidence, we have chosen chairs close to Dr. Ashfaq Ishaq, an official of the International Child Art Foundation who, for many years, has organized the World Children's Festival. A couple days ago, I spoke briefly on the phone to him about the children's visa problem and today we both express gratitude that the problem is solved.

Of course Margaret and I are ready to cheer the Ugandan children but where are they? We listen to explosive song expressions from Maori children of New Zealand and singing Swedish teenagers being accompanied by two violinists. We watch and listen to a number of performing groups. But, where are the Ugandans?

When they do arrive and begin singing, we and the entire audience are MESMERIZED! Of primary interest is that they sing with their hearts open with love. Strong voices, positive words. Yes, they should receive an award!

Well, we saw no awards given to anyone while we were at the festival. Later, Mike emails saying that at the evening banquet, three awards were given to outstanding figures. He won an award for mobilizing the biggest and best music performance group.

Hurray! Hurray!

CHAPTER 2

SEDONA JOURNEY

From Barbara:

Sedona is a place where I could live forever. It's atmosphere is 'angelic', peaceful, and at the same time, stimulating. The energy is incredible and it doesn't turn on and off. It stays on.

Sedona sits amid gorgeous scenery of red rock that towers mightily and stretches for miles and miles and miles. Its history goes back millions of years, and the majestic red rock mountains display the area's history. Much of the red rock remains without vegetation, and so one can look at these red mountains and see a change in rock formation where Mother Earth has changed her way of living and where another way begins.

Can you imagine looking at these mountains and seeing this?

As I am writing you, I have in front of me a big Sedona pamphlet called 2015-2016 Official Visitor's Guide whose front cover has a photograph of a gorgeous red rock landscape stretching miles and miles.

Why have we chosen to go to Sedona this June? We will attend the Kryon Summer Light Conference at the Sedona Red Rock High

School auditorium. This is a summit meeting called "The Birth of a New Earth Consciousness". Twelve channelers will gather to speak to the audience.

Yes, this conference interests us, and so Margaret and I will be part of the audience.

June 4:

This morning, 4:15 a.m., Joan the taxi driver picks us up to take us to the airport so we can take Delta Airlines to Detroit, transfer, and fly to Phoenix. On landing, we will be renting a Hertz car to drive to Sedona.

It is always fun to ride along with Joan who, even at this early hour, is alert and talkative. We three are soon laughing and cracking jokes.

On arrival at the airport, because we have earlier printed out our boarding passes, we can go directly to Security which gives us no delays. Then it is only a matter of waiting for the plane to leave. And yes, we do leave on time, and we arrive in Detroit on time.

Our Delta plane to Phoenix leaves at 8:43 a.m. and we arrive in Phoenix at 9:43 a.m., Phoenix time. A short ride, yes, but, our New York watches tell us that we have flown three hours more than what the Phoenix clock tells us.

On arrival, we note that the temperature in Phoenix is 95 degrees Fahrenheit. We should feel hot, but the humidity is low and so, to us, the temperature feels more like 75 degrees Fahrenheit.

A quick shuttle ride to Car Rentals soon has us renting a Hertz car, and we are given a shiny, black car that looks like it has just been driven off the assembly line. Is it a new car? It sure looks like a new car. In fact, it is so new, we have to be taught the system for starting it. Put a foot on the brake and then push a button on the dashboard before the car will start. We have other new items to learn about this car.

It has a GPS guidance system which a Hertz employee programs to direct us from the Phoenix airport to our hotel in Sedona. Well, the woman inside this GPS guidance system has a mind of her own, and her first instruction for leaving the rental car area is to turn to the right. Hertz has told us to turn to the left. Who is right, the woman or Hertz?

We follow the woman's instructions and within a minute or two, we realize we are going in the wrong direction to reach Expressway 17 North, our route to Sedona.

Well, woman, you have started off on the wrong foot with us.

We correct our driving to reach Expressway 17 North, and we are soon on it and moving along steadily with traffic that does not behave hysterically. Good! Because the car is new and unfamiliar to us, Margaret, who is driving, drives slowly.

After a time, unexpectedly, the GPS woman makes a comment about being in a particular lane and we realize she is correct.

Okay, woman, maybe you have decided to speak correctly to us.

We go along feeling as if Phoenix stretches its arms out forever, but finally we are driving in countryside with few homes and other buildings. I remember when I was a child and my parents drove me and my sisters through unpopulated Montana land that had light poles with antelope standing in the scarce shade of the poles.

Do I see any antelope today? No. Suddenly I miss them.

I do not see any grazing animals on this journey. Not even grazing animals at farms. Maybe they live and eat in barns.

When we are coming close to Sedona, we see signs for Route 250 and we know this is the route we must take to Route 89A that will take us to our destination.

Will the woman agree? No.

Well, woman, you can jump from your GPS box and go your own way and we will go our way.

When we do reach 89A, she makes no comment until a few miles further along when she tells us to go on a road that has nothing to do with reaching Sedona! I have thoughts of people listening to a GPS box woman and they have wandered around until they are high in the mountains or out of gas in the middle of nowhere.

In any case, we do arrive in Sedona, and, to our DELIGHTFUL SURPRISE, the hotel where we will be staying, Days Inn, is on 89A! We come to it without realizing we would be coming to it.

Hurray!

As for the GPS woman, when we reach our hotel, we turn her off and she will stay off permanently throughout our entire journey.

Interesting, when we make comments in Sedona about this GPS woman, we learn that we have not been the only ones who have been given misleading information. Apparently, GPS can be programed to unexpectedly take people high up into the mountains and elsewhere. Well, we do have an interest in seeing the mountains of Sedona, but we wish to see them on our own terms. Meaning, we can view them from the base rather than from the top.

I am excited to begin viewing millions and millions of years of Mother Earth's red rock staring me in the face, but we need to drive a bit further to have a good look. Now it is time to check into the hotel, take our suitcases out of the car, put them in the room, find a place to eat, and then collapse for the remainder of the day. Tomorrow, the mountains will be 'spoken' to.

The hotel man at the front desk gives us the name of a pizza restaurant and we easily drive a few minutes to this place. And yes, it is a friendly place and we enjoy talking with our waitress. She brings us open fire pizza and we are eating it when a sudden storm with lightning arrives. One sharp blast of lightning and the restaurant power fails.

Well, we have our pizza and we continue eating as we listen to remarks about earlier power failures in Sedona. No one seems alarmed. Only patient. I hear that storms have been striking this place often in the past months, and the electricity quits.

What is this all about????

When we leave the restaurant, the electricity has not returned. I am thinking that Mother Earth has a consciousness as well as the red rocks of gigantic mountains here at Sedona. There is no 'death' of consciousness. In ancient times, Mother Earth was not endowed with negative energies, nor were the red rocks of the Sedona mountains. She wore only positive energies, and all who lived on her wore positive energies. They remain with positive energies.

I believe that negative actions of humanity can occasionally put a small dent into Sedona, such as a quick storm, but this will only be temporary. THE POSITIVE ENERGIES ARE POWERFUL and they will remain. It is understandable to me that artists and writers gather here to live at this powerful energy place. It is also understandable to me that the Kryon Summer Light Conference is here. I am excited to attend!

June 5:

Our plan is to spend the day looking at Sedona and the mountains. Tomorrow we will attend the conference, and the next day.

This morning, after a good night's sleep, we have a delightful breakfast with other hotel residents and then we climb into our shiny black rental car to begin our first destination for the day -- the Chapel of the Holy Cross, home of Mother Mary. Years ago, I visited this place, and it is indeed holy.

As we begin driving, we first must travel along Route 89A through the city itself, and I note how much more 'grown up' this place is. Many, many more shops and buildings than when I was here over fifteen years ago.

Well, one has to expect growth and I am pleased the city feels comfortable. Much is here for tourists, and their energies are not spoiling the landscape.

When we turn from Route 89A to Route 179, I begin looking for Chapel Road which will take us to Mary's place, and yes, we do easily see the sign for Chapel Road. Now we will begin driving a bit upward until the road becomes steeper, and this means we are close to the Chapel.

Yes! Here are parking spots for cars, and we choose one, park the car, and begin walking upward toward a lookout place that is just below the Chapel.

Few people are here this morning, and in fact, when we reach the lookout place, we have it to ourselves.

And now I am disappointed. I vividly remember the last time I looked out and down at what is before us. A wide, wide area that years ago looked like the remnants of a wide river. Not today. Houses and houses and houses are built here, and many, many trees are growing.

In ancient times, dolphins used to swim where I am looking, and when the great shift came and the water rushed out, good-bye home of the dolphins. My memory showed me this the last time I was here. Well, not today!

Now Margaret and I are turning away from the lookout place to take a concrete walkway upward to the Chapel itself. When we are nearly at the Chapel entrance, we come to a tiny fountain beside a small cluster of cultivated, multi-colored flowers that look happy. We pause to put a speck of healing water here before entering Mary's Chapel.

And yes, I am happy because the energy inside is exactly the same as the positive energy of years ago when I was here. Good!

This is not a big place, and I think anyone entering will feel comfortable regardless of one's religious attitude. There is no attempt here to put pressure on anyone.

This morning, less than a half-dozen are here and we have nearly the whole place to ourselves. I sit in the front row and just ahead of me to my left are many lighted candles. If I counted them, and I do not, I think there are fifty lighted candles.

As I am sitting, two women come to light candles to acknowledge Mary. It is their tradition to do this, and probably they are asking for help with a personal problem, or a problem within the family, or maybe a world problem.

Yes, this place is comfortable. One can feel many unseen entities here. This small place feels loaded with them.

When I leave, I look at the red mountain just behind this Chapel. Here is where the Pleiadians land their craft. Do they enter the Chapel? Probably not.

Sedona is a place where a number of off-world entities land their spacecraft. Well, why not? The energies are good. One would want to land in good energies.

Now it is time to put my mind on the next stop, Bell Rock. It is close to the Mary Chapel, on the same road, and we go along looking at Bell Rock as our little black shiny car takes us on Route 179 which has been rebuilt since my last journey here. Now it is like an expressway divided by land and vegetation so that the southbound lanes cannot be seen by the northbound lanes.

We have no problem finding a way to cross to the other side of the expressway, and we are soon at a parking area to leave cars when walking to Bell Rock Mountain. However, we do not want to walk to Bell Rock Mountain. We want the mountain to be within a few feet of our car. This was possible years ago, before the expressway was built. I remember getting out of a car and walking maybe one minute to the bottom edge of the mountain holding Bell Rock, which, incidentally, is a huge rock perched on the top of the mountain.

We stop the car in the parking lot and we look at Bell Rock. Years ago, and maybe now, this was the place where a Cosmic Council would meet. I do not feel any activity at this place.

Well, I am happy to see this place again, and I am also happy to see red Cathedral Rock and the group of towering red rocks gathered together far across the way but easily viewed from here.

Visiting Tlaquepaque Village is next on the list of viewing, and it is reached by returning on Route 179 to almost Route 89A. Its name is impossible to pronounce correctly and I am understanding that it stems from the Mexican word describing a traditional village that has the best of everything.

The Tlaquepaque Village we will be visiting is noted for its arts and crafts, and here we will be seeing artists at work as well as many specialty shops and art galleries.

When we enter this place, we park facing wind sculptures, all different, all moving gracefully with the wind. It is REMARKABLE what we are seeing. We soon learn that their maker, Lyman Whitaker, has visited Antarctica and erected a huge sundial at the South Pole. He dedicates his sculpting to the wind and weather and he wants his work to inspire love for the wind from people who see his work.

*See Glossary: Lyman Whitaker.

Well, he certainly has caught our attention! I would LOVE one of his sculptures.

We are directed to a place to eat no more than fifty feet from the wind sculptures, and after our meal, we realize that across the way is the gallery of artist Bearcloud who is our friend! We have been wondering where in Sedona his gallery is located, and here it is. Amazing! We enter and he has just arrived. Thank you, whoever has helped arrange this unexpected meeting!

*See Glossary: Bearcloud.

When we leave him, we drive about seven minutes to the Sedona Heritage Museum to check the background of this place. And yes, the museum has the background of first White settlers to Sedona, but the concentration is not on Native Americans who used to live here. Well, one can't see everything.

After viewing what the museum has to offer, we are done for the day. Tired. Tomorrow will begin an all-day session at the Kryon Summer Light Conference.

But rather than begin writing you about tomorrow's conference, I want to tell you that about a week ago the Internet announced that Sunset Crater at Flagstaff has shown signs of becoming active. It has been quiet a long time, and we do not want any activity now. And so, while we are in Sedona, we drive Route 89A to reach Flagstaff.

This is not a long drive and the scenery is MAGNIFICANT. Few are taking this road and so we can drive slowly and look at the mighty mountains on either side of the road. When we arrive at Flagstaff, it is easy enough to find Sunset Crater and we feel there is no indication that there is activity. Interesting, just above are three small white clouds in a blue, cloudless sky. Are these three small white clouds hiding Pleiadian spacecraft?

June 6, Saturday:

Today will be a full day of attending the Kryon Summer Light Conference. As mentioned earlier, it is at the Sedona Red Rock High School auditorium, and that is easy enough to find. It is on Route 89A about two miles from our hotel, and we will be passing it when we return to Phoenix.

This is a huge high school. It is 'out of town' and so my thought is that it accommodates students from all over Sedona. There are no other buildings sitting nearby. It is by itself.

We arrive early Saturday morning because we have learned that many will be coming to the conference, and we know this means there will be many cars. The parking lots will be full. And so we have arrived early to find a place to park, and we do.

What can I say about this conference?

Channeling from Archangel Michael via Ronna Herman explains that a huge Soul Family Group is being created to provide a force that will help the world change to loving thoughts. Millions are in the process of Ascension which means millions are involved with the process of higher awareness.

Each, as a Master of his own destiny, must discern how this is to be done and not merely to follow mindlessly other's thoughts. Each must create thoughts of beauty and harmony.

I am taking seriously what Archangel Michael says about each being a Master of his own destiny. What is to be done is in the hands of the individual.

Here is a comment that Lee Carroll has channeled from Kryon. A new energy is becoming available that will change the consciousness. However, one is urged to not take this comment at 'face value'. There is a need for the mind to discern what has been said.

On the stage of the conference is a Stargate for anyone to enter. And yes, many do.

*See Glossary: The Stargate Experience.

What is this Stargate?

It is a device created by Englishman Prageet to open inter-dimensional doorways to higher consciousness. And, since all on Mother Earth, whether or not this is known, are being directed to dimensions higher than the third dimension, this Stargate can help quicken Ascension. Its energy field has the ability resonate with an individual's energy field to help bring about change so that abilities and skills dormant within the individual can be awakened. The multidimensional abilities of the Stargate attract high Beings, such as the Nature Spirits, the Angelic Beings, and Star Beings who, by way of the Stargate, can assist those wishing to Ascend.

Yes, this is a very interesting conference. We sit listening for hours and hours with a full auditorium and no one wants to leave.

When the conference is over, we return the rental car to Phoenix, and then we fly back to New York State. Surprisingly, we learn that musician Paul Winter has recently visited the Grand Canyon where he composed music for the June Solstice event at the Cathedral of St. John the Divine in New York City.

We write him to say we have just returned from Sedona which has the same frequencies as the Grand Canyon, and he immediately emails that we should speak to him after the Solstice performance.

The Grand Canyon is a deep canyon 277 miles long and at least 5,000 feet deep. Some geologists consider it to be two billion years old. And yes, like the Sedona mountains, it has positive energies because it came into being while Mother Earth only had positive energies. BECAUSE OF ITS SIZE, THINK HOW POWERFUL THESE POSITIVE ENERGIES ARE!

Then we learn from David Adams of Australia, who regularly channels, that at the Solstice, Mother Earth receives a new Cosmic frequency of Light to lift her from being the Blue Planet to one called the Magenta Planet, the planet of love and peace!

Paul Winter brings to the Solstice the powerful positive energies of the Grand Canyon and we will bring to the Solstice from Sedona the powerful energies that are just up the road from the Grand Canyon.

Wow! What a privilege to be there! Magenta Light comes within our hearts and allows us to be lifted into the Soul Dimension of Mother Earth where we begin new journeys. New frequencies, new vibrations, new dimensions of Light.

And a P.S. to all this: When we meet Paul Winter at the cathedral, he is wearing a shirt the color of deep magenta.

Chapter 3

Sedona Journey

From Margaret:

June 3, the day before we leave for Sedona, Arizona, to attend The Masters Channeling Summit conference, on the computer we see steam plumes coming from the Sunset Crater volcanic complex less than fifty miles from Sedona. This has been dormant a long time and so we worry. We don't want activity in dormant craters.

June 4, 6:10 a.m. we take an early flight to Detroit where we transfer to a Phoenix-bound flight leaving at 8:40 a.m. When we are flying over the midsection of the country, a thick cloud mass is below us. Breaks in the clouds show us some land flooding.

While coming into the Phoenix area, I am thinking of sacred Sedona close by. I have my Vortex book of symbols with me and I want to send this Vortex energy not only to the Sedona-Phoenix area but to the entire world. I begin silently reading and tracing the symbols with my finger, focusing on the Universal Law of Light, Sound and Vibration, Intuition and Future Sight, etc.

*See Glossary: Vortex Symbols.

At 9:43 a.m. Arizona time, we arrive in Phoenix, and this timing is astonishing because we have been flying a long time, not just one hour. However, Arizona has a three-hour time difference from the East Coast.

We rent a car to drive to Sedona. At first there is heavy traffic and then it thins and we move quickly. I am driving and my heart begins reacting physically because ancient waters used to be here, and I am thinking of the dolphins that were swimming here. The land is displaying all colors -- black volcanic boulders – red, white, pinks, rose, blue, violet, all the colors of the Painted Desert. Finally, near Sedona the color is mostly red.

The crows, the ravens, and black beautiful flyers greet us. An antelope appears in a split moment where the different dimensions open up. Snakes, rattlers are here. Their presence means to honor the snake, the closest to Mother Earth that feels every ripple of her energy.

I receive a message: *To enter the area, you must have a heart of Lightness, Sweetness, Trueness. A heart of projecting Love frequency.*

As I am approaching Sedona, my heart is full of Love. I know all hearts react the same. Mother Earth's heart is on the surface. I do not have to go underground to tap into her. She is present. She is powerful. That is why Sedona is such a magnet for people to come.

When we arrive in Sedona we quickly reach our hotel, Day's Inn, where we are given an excellent room by a kind attendant. In the afternoon this same attendant suggests we eat dinner at Lisa Pizza. While eating, a great electrical windstorm comes up and the power goes off. We note that all the people are calm and we listen to a waitress talking to a friend about energy lines here in Sedona. She says present times are changing and planetary configurations are helping humanity. When she adds she is totally attuned and will strive to do her best, the listener nods her head in agreement. We listen while eating pizza and arugula salad with goat cheese, pie nuts, artichoke hearts, eggplants and onions.

When the storm clears and I am still at the restaurant, I enjoy a magnificent view of Thunder Mountain, vast and complex.

June 5:

3:30 a.m., I receive channeling:

Music is here. Love is here. Electricity is here. Magnetism is here. Iron, copper, the minerals are here with their gifts and consequences. Choose wisely, they say. Greed and impatience cannot be here. Anger. Short-sightedness cannot be here in the presence of the eternal stone mass mountains. Layers and layers of realities. Seas come. Seas go. Volcanoes come alive to vent, to close, to sleep, to come alive again.

Arizona is all about water – the presence, the absence. It is always present in the living here. Storms come and go. Rain falls onto many levels. Erosion – the sculptor – the realities are here. So many are here with you. The Angelic presence. The Guardians of the Nature Kingdoms. The Brothers and Sisters of other worlds. They are all joining in the gathering of the Summer Light Conference. All come to unite and share and send out this energy to the planet and to the universe. Let this be a grand time, a grand reunion.

Just now above Sunset Crater, steam plumes are appearing. The volcanoes are becoming awakened again to appear on the surface in steam and heat.

Times are quickening. What took decades, centuries to appear, now takes days, weeks, months, years. Time is changing. Realities thinning. Keep your being (your four bodies and beyond) balanced and refined. All in harmony. You cannot swim thrashing around in the water. The Dolphins are here. Walk with a wide-open lens, wide-angle camera. Examine and receive all the different layers and realities. If magma comes closer to the surface, then the steam plumes remove the pressure. How happily everyone walked around Yellowstone to see Old Faithful and the other geysers. Now the full reality has become apparent. Steam release, harmony release in sound as in the old and new steam calliopes. May your thoughts be of the highest frequency. The thought layer on Mother Earth reflects and affects the internal state of the planet. All are important. The ant, the snake, the dolphin, the whale, the fox, the coyote, the deer, the elk, the buffalo, the hummingbird, the eagle, the hawk, the butterfly, and the rocks. All are important. The humans need to see how they fit in – not to damage and rearrange Mother Earth's surface, but to be one with her and with the others in full consciousness of Earth's reality which is pumping out in headlines wide-screen messages from the rock layers of the majestic presence and being of Sedona. Magnificent. Simple. Direct. Complex. All and all. Far beyond your imagination and comprehension. And directly available. Go for it.

From The Guardian Guide of Sedona Frequency.

In the early morning, I read my notes to Barbara and rest again with the curtain open to look at a tall pine tree. Native Americans say we are in the time cycle of the Moon of the Tree which is the Guardian of the Spiritual Law of Equality, rising through the dimensions and realities in an equal, balanced way.

*See Glossary: The Symbols as well as the EarthStar Calendar.

We have brought with us special healing water for all of Nature, and after sunrise, I take the water to a white blooming bush growing close to our room. It is so fragrant and it is enjoying the sunlight pouring in from the east. The day has dawned brilliantly.

After breakfast, we drive to Mary's Chapel which merges into a red rock mountain. I feel Her presence. We stop here and face east where once the view was of an ancient sea where the dolphins swam. Sacred Bell Rock is in the distance.

We walk up a suspended walkway to a fountain of Mary where we give love and a bit of healing water to the fountain and flowers. The flowers respond by shining brightly. Now we enter the church and it feels good to be here. We stay for a time.

When we leave, we drive close to towering Bell Rock where Galactic Councils meet. We stop and sound the OM's for planetary peace. Peace on Earth. Peace above and beyond. And, we place healing water on plants.

Our next stop is Tlaquepaque, an artist community of galleries and shops where we enter a photographic gallery showing bright images of Sedona. Then we enter another a shop of fossils and crystals. Here we have an amazing encounter with the shopkeeper who is writing a book on healing. Our stories are parallel and our viewpoints are the same. We give her a book knowing we will continue to be in touch.

Outside, we view metal wind sculptures moving and dancing in the wind, created by Lyman Whitaker, whose work captures Nature's geometry in motion. The sculptures dance and expand in different shapes and sizes. This art is a wonder to behold!

Suddenly we see Bearcloud Gallery and we rush inside to find our friend working on his computer which is giving him a dilemma. We give him love and greetings and Barbara sends positive energy to his computer. Later, when we return to give him our book, 2014 And Beyond, his computer is just fine. A magical encounter.

June 6:

3:30 a.m. rough night sleeping. A thunderstorm is in the distance. I think of the origin of the name of Sedona. It was the name of the wife of the Post Master who had to name the place where mail was to be delivered in 1902.

Two other names had been rejected. For me, the history of Sedona is held in the rock layers that are vast and dramatic with great movements over time.

I receive channeling:

Rest on top and within this power place which recharges everyone who visits. Sedona is a recharging base for everyone -- all the surface, inside, above and within. Find your frequency, match and you are there. Part of the many layers of complexity. Sedona complexity. Sedona smooth. Sedona abrupt. Sedona vast. Sedona love magnetics always pulling you to return.

The Guardian of the Frequencies of the Sedona Spirit.

This morning we still have time before the conference begins to do more 'sight-seeing'. We want to see more of the mountains, and so we take the Upper Red Rock Loop Road and see a spectacular view of Cathedral Rock. It is a perfect, clear day and the sun is shining on the rocks. We have a clear view of the rock formations as we follow the winding road.

When we reach the road to the airport which is high up, we begin seeing a magnificent view of Thunder Mountain. We park high up and I take with me healing water to the bushes and pine tree clusters, guardians of the land. I give water to all the plants and they are happy.

When we begin returning to a lower level, Barbara has the idea to drive to the area of Sunset Crater to see if there are plumes of steam. We have learned about that before coming to Sedona and we know that these plumes of steam could be coming from an ancient volcano now active.

When we are at the base of the mountains, we drive along Oak Creek toward Flagstaff. The view is breath-taking. And now our road takes us up again to a pine forest. Our roadmap shows we are now on our way into Flagstaff where we should be able to find Sunset Crater. Yes, we do and it seems calm and settled with snow on top of the mountain. We see no plumes and we feel relief. We send blessings to the land and return to Sedona.

And now we turn our attention to the conference in a large auditorium filled with those who have come to hear well-known channelers. Ronna Herman is here. James Tyberonn is here. Fred Sterling. We sit and listen attentively to them speaking on a wide stage before us. They sit mainly on the left and on the right side is a large metal structure called a Stargate.

It has been explained to us that this structure is a doorway to higher worlds and the audience is invited to come on stage and walk within this structure. It is about 8 feet high. Barbara and I accept this invitation and we briefly stand within the structure. But, we realize that too many are trying to do this at the same time and so it is best to return to our seats and visit later.

*See Glossary: The Stargate Experience.

I should note here that I bought a special star crystal from Ronna Herman. Later, I receive a message from Archangel Michael about this crystal.

Get out your crystal you have so carefully put away. You see it has many facets. Five star, six star. The light is strong at every point. Aspect point, balance point, expansion, soul emerging. Consider yourself in the star crystal reaching out, expanding, sending out the frequency of Love, peace and harmony. You are ever expanding in Light. You are unique and yet merged with others. You realize you are a water bearer bringing the messages of the Being of Water.

The time of sunset is here when the bright sun dips into the darkness to dawn the new day at another part of the planet. Bless the day. Thank Mother Earth for your journey.

He continues:

The crystal you have is connected to your angelic helpers. Be aware of their presence. You felt my presence. We are here with those who seek perfection on Mother Earth whose essence is harmony and balance.

Sedona is a hard place to leave because the dimensions are merged into one. There is no difficulty in sliding, merging with the All. When the conference people leave Sedona, they will send out their strong force field of Love. Each person comes away with a new perspective and new clarity.

Ever present is my love for humanity. I am Archangel Michael. I seem distant but I am close up.

———————————————

Before we leave the conference, Barbara and I return to the Stargate, which is actually called The Stargate Experience. Where I enter, I can feel the words, *Welcome to the Portal.* I know this new entry into my life will continue, and yes, we buy a small Stargate to help us with our work of healing Mother Earth and all who live on her.

On stage close to the Stargate is a big flower arrangement. On the other side of the stage near the podium where announcements are made about the program is another flower arrangement. On the last day of the conference, I note that the flowers next to the podium are wilted. On the Stargate side the flowers seem to flourish and stand brightly in their radiance. I am thinking of the power of the Stargate and I receive a message.

Use the Stargate portal to heal the water. Look at the vibrancy of the flowers in the water next to the Stargate.

I think of the need to heal the Pacific, all the water of the world, and I receive a message: *Tools. Use tools for healing what is not right with Mother Earth and her life forms.*

Angelic presence: We will enhance and direct your expanded understanding.

With my love to all humanity and all life forms on Mother Earth. Archangel Michael

June 8-9:

The conference is over and we drive to Phoenix, turn in the car and begin putting our minds on flying East the next day.

We board a flight to Atlanta and are settled down peacefully, accepting this long flight when suddenly we realize the plane is going in the opposite direction. The stewardess tells us there is a severe thunder and lightning storm in Atlanta and we must go into a holding pattern. However, after a time we are told the plane is running out of fuel and we must land immediately in either Knoxville or Asheville. But no, we need to land now! Our plane begins coasting down to a runway in Huntsville, Alabama. Wow, we are happy to be on the ground safely!

While this dire situation is happening, I get out the Vortexes and pray for Movement and Balance, Nature, and Love and Healing. I put the Vortex booklet to my chest, holding it tight, sending out love and calming energies around the plane and over the area.

It is late afternoon in Huntsville and we land in clear, golden Light. After receiving fuel, we take off again and the sky becomes strange colors of orange, pink, red, blue, dark grey. Eerie colors. We see massive storm clouds which the pilot avoids, and in thirty minutes we are at the Atlanta terminal. Everyone is relieved we all landed safely. Now we are with stranded passengers seeking flights. Everyone is calm and polite with kindness and compassion for each other.

This has been a powerful trip from beginning to end.

CHAPTER 4

MOUNT SHASTA JOURNEY

F rom Barbara:

August 7:

This morning Joan the taxi driver sends an early call so we will be ready for her transportation to the airport to catch planes headed toward California.

Why are we going in California? To visit Mount Shasta, considered to be one of the most powerful places on the continent. I call Mount Shasta 'she', although others will call her 'he'. She is multidimensional, which is important during this time of Ascension when humanity is moving from the third to the fifth dimension. Her energy is powerful, which can make one light-headed and even stagger a bit when one arrives within her influence.

4:15 a.m., lights from Joan's taxi tells us she is ready to take us to the airport, and we grab our bags to join her. She is alert, as if it is the middle of the day, and we ride along joking with her and having a good time. When I ask her what time she left her bed to drive us to the airport, she says she has not yet been to bed. Wow! I think I would be no good as a taxi driver.

At the airport, we wheel our bags through Security with our boarding passes in hand thanks to the airlines that sent them yesterday via email. The computer does have its advantages!

Our 6 a.m. flight to Chicago is full and it gets us off the ground on time. The sun is awake and up and we watch the land as we move along. Then the clouds come in and the pilot takes us above them. I think these are strange clouds. They look more like big chunks of white stuff stuck together. What happened to normal looking clouds?

At Chicago, we dip below these chunks and land at big O'Hare airport called ORD. Why that name? In any case, we are here at this big, big, big airport, and when we learn our next flight leaves at 'the other end' of the airport, we have a long way to transfer to reach our 9:05 flight to the San Francisco airport, called SFO. Here is the use of the 'O' again. What does it mean?

On our plane to SFO, we sit next to a man who seems to have lived his life as a fireman. We start talking and he says when he was old enough to begin thinking about quitting his life-time work, the government hires him to find ways to prevent or stop fires in different parts of the country. At the moment he is on his way to northeastern California to try to find a way to stop out-of-control fires in a wilderness area that has many sequoia trees. I hope he is successful!

At San Francisco, we transfer to a plane leaving for Medford, Oregon at 12:46 p.m., and this destination is called MFR. Why the R? An 'O' could stand for Oregon.

When we reach Medford, we have been traveling eleven hours and eleven minutes, or 2,703 miles. Well, that was fast enough. We survived even without food which the airlines would prefer not to think about.

At Medford we rent a new, little Nissan car, dark grey, and after we learn how to open the locked doors when we stop the car to get out, we begin driving close to two hours to Mount Shasta City where we will stay one week.

As we drive along, we comment about the weather which looks strange. It is hazy with thick particles coming from fire, and we wonder how people with lung problems could breathe properly. We do not have lung problems, but we keep the car windows closed and the air conditioning on.

When we come close to Mount Shasta City, we see in the distance Mount Shasta herself. I am surprised. She looks naked. She has only a few strips of white snow on her extensive brown skin. When one opens the Internet and sees her photograph, she is wearing a big white coat of snow.

How can this woman show herself as naked? Here, as we are driving along, I am beginning to see females wearing colorful clothes. Yes, Madame Shasta needs more color. With my mind, I drape her with a colorful shawl of blue sapphire.

At Mount Shasta City we have no difficulty finding the Alpine Lodge where we have already booked a room for the week. Here, we will meet our friend Carmen Balhestero of Sao Paulo, Brazil. She and her group of Brazilians will be staying here.

*See Glossary: Carmen Balhestero.

We know Carmen has returned to this same location for years and years, and always at this same time. She is closely associated with Saint Germain who, every year at this time gives her via channeling information about work she will be doing this coming year.

A few years ago in Brazil when we were visiting her, Carmen was rapidly channeling Saint Germain for a Portuguese-speaking gathering when suddenly she began speaking rapidly in English. A message from St. Germain was coming in to tell us to use everything to do our work, including elementals. This was a surprise, and, actually, we did begin bringing in elementals to help with the work.

Well, we know Carmen is here at Mount Shasta City with her group and they are staying at the Alpine Lodge. When we meet, we hug each other with joy.

Margaret and I are hungry and Carmen tells us the best restaurant is a two-minute walk from the Alpine Lodge. We say good-bye for the moment to walk to the Lilys Restaurant where we enter and take a seat next to a table of diners just being served. We see their portions are HUGE, and we quickly decide to order one serving and split it between the two of us. Would the waiter agree? Yes.

When we do eat, we agree with those who think this is the best restaurant in town. Wow!

August 8:

8, 8, 8 --- This is the day of the '8's.

2015 is added to make 8; the next 8 comes from the 8th month of the year, and next is the 8th day of the month. This is also the moment when the planet Venus becomes retrograde by turning her face toward her sister planet Earth. Venus features are those of the Divine Feminine, the giver of Love, the giver of Life.

Saint Germain has told Carmen to go to Hedge Creek Falls today for the honoring of the Divine Feminine and we will be with her later this morning. As for the beginning of our day, Margaret has taken the little Nissan on an exploration journey to find a place for us to eat breakfast. And yes, she has found a perfect place, called the Black Bear Diner.

The drive from Alpine Lodge to the Black Bear Diner is only a couple minutes, and we are soon parking our Nissan in their parking lot which is nearly full. It is only about 7 a.m. on a Saturday morning. What happened to weekend sleep-ins? In any case, we take the last parking spot and then enter the Black Bear Diner to wait in line for a table. Packed. This place is packed. Well, this must mean the food is mighty good.

When we are given a table, we sit and look at two thin newspapers on the table in front of us. The Black Bear Gazette dated 1962. The front page features American Astronaut John Glenn orbiting the earth, and the second feature is an article about Redding driver Bob McGrath breaking the speed record at Bonneville, wherever that is. He comments that the 250 mile-per-hour ride was a fast one.

When our waiter, order pad in hand, asks us if we are ready to order, we comment that the menu has not yet arrived. He opens The Black Bear Gazette and the inside is our menu.

Wow! There are many selections!

Now we learn that this Black Bear Diner is the first Black Bear Diner and there are now over sixty more across the land. Well, I can understand why the number has grown and grown and it will continue to grow. Excellent food, attentive waiters, excellent service!

The owners, Sugar Bear and Papa Bear, wanted to give people a place to eat that reminded them of home and good food.

Well, I certainly agree they have succeeded in giving us both first class treatment and first class food!

After filling ourselves with 'family food', Margaret and I are ready to explore this wonderful area called Mount Shasta, and we begin with Hedge Creek Falls only a stone's throw from the activity of Mount Shasta City. For me, 'town' would seem to be a better word, but never mind.

We go to the falls area with Carmen's group, and when we reach the descending pathway from the road to the falls, we begin walking downward. Saint Germain has told Carmen how important Hedge

Creek Falls is from an esoteric standpoint, and he soon gives Carmen a message in Portuguese. Margaret and I listen with the others but we do not understand.

Around us is a forest of stately, towering trees. Friendly trees. One cannot help but pet them as we walk along. Margaret begins putting down vortex symbols at the foot of the trees. No one is in a rush to leave this place.

After a time, though, Margaret and I begin walking back to the road, and when we are nearly there, we see an elderly man sitting alone on a bench. Beside him is a paperback book with an esoteric title. To me, this man does not seem to be the type who would be reading such a book, and I stop and say hello to him. He 'hellos' back. When I ask if he has walked downhill to reach the falls, he shakes his head to indicate no and I realize his mental body may want to reach the falls, but his physical body is unable. I ask if I can sit beside him and his book for a moment and he nods yes.

We begin talking about this magic place, and in the course of talking, I glance down at the book between us, and I casually ask if his family agrees with this book. He shakes his head no and I realize he is a loner whose only company are his thoughts. Well, just now, here comes Carmen's folks from Hedge Creek Falls and so we say good-bye to this pleasant man who has nothing but his book to entertain him.

Margaret and I will be visiting several sacred waterways, and one complex is called McCloud River, Lower, Middle and Upper Falls. It is the weekend, and when we reach this complex, we stand above the falls and watch families wearing bright-colored swimsuits in the water below us. What a beautiful day it is! Warm -- neither too hot or too cold. We have brought swimsuits with us to Shasta but we do not have them with us today.

Around us is a gorgeous forest of trees, and for a time we sit at a picnic table looking at the forest paradise around us and the swimmers below us.

I need to mention here that we also visited the headwaters of the Sacramento River located in Mount Shasta City Park. We had no idea what to expect. Is this headwaters a big place?

No. Not at all. In fact, it is merely a trickle of water seeming to come out of nowhere, but actually from the Klamath Mountains. At the source of the Sacramento River, I kneel down, put my hands in the water, scoop it up and drink it. Wow! What an experience! The largest river in California begins here and runs 445 miles south before reaching San Francisco Bay.

I watch people coming to the source of the Sacramento River to fill their jugs with this sacred, healthy water. Would Margaret and I be allowed to take it on an airplane when we leave Mount Shasta? Probably not.

Stewart Mineral Springs a few miles outside of Mount Shasta City also catches our attention, and we drive here to experience this water famous for its many minerals and other attributes that penetrate the taste and bring healthy delight to the cells of the body.

I can understand why people have come to Mount Shasta to reside 'forever'. Our bodies, after all, are about eighty percent water. To give the cells fresh, healthy water every day would probably bring cheers from them.

Now it is time tell you about our journey to a pageant of angels and a choir concert of sacred music yearly performed twice at Mount Shasta City at this time of year. We also see a Christ pageant performed twice at this time of year. The amphitheater is outside and holds about 1000 people who sit quietly watching the performances. My feeling is that many return yearly to see the performances.

By prearrangement, we visit the home of well-known musician Anton Mizerak to listen to him playing the harmonica, synthesizers, piano, and classical Indian drums called the tabla. His home is perched on

Mount Shasta, and we feel strongly the influence of his wonderful music from this mystical place.

Will we forget what we experienced at Mount Shasta? No.

There is need to tell you about the drive to the top of Mount Shasta, a very special drive. The road is generous for cars and I am thinking that the authorities who designed and who continue to maintain this road have kept their thoughts on many, many cars that will use this road.

At the beginning of the drive, trees stand tall and firm like sentries on both sides of the road. One feels like saluting them. As we amble along looking at the magnificent scenery of green forest, we see are all sizes of trees. Some are very small but stand stately like their parents whose seeds have reached the ground to sprout the newcomers.

At one place, rather high up, is an extensive area of brown dirt and we realize that a landslide has brought down the trees. Little ones are beginning to come up, and in time, the landslide will be a matter of the past.

It has been pointed out to us that trees, mostly pine, provide food for the deer, of which we see a few. Also, we learn that the pines can provide food for hungry humans because the new growth is edible. And, if one sees a tall pine covered with a light green, like moss, this tree is preparing to die. The moss is edible, and so, if one is caught in the forest with no food, the moss can be a lifesaver.

As mentioned earlier, Mount Shasta has much more than the physical to attract visitors here. Its energy field is extensive, and the dimensions are many. Doors open for those who recognize what is here.

And, it is open to our brothers and sisters living on the homelands of Sirius, the Pleiades, Arcturus, and other places. Yes, there are many different interests for paying attention to this sacred place. From an energy standpoint, Mount Shasta is a triangular, double pyramid with one point at the top and the other at the bottom.

Everything has a consciousness including the trees in a forest and the flowers in a garden. Mount Shasta has a consciousness. If this is understood, then there is a possibility of connecting to ancient people living in the fifth dimension within Mount Shasta in a place called Telos. They have been living here a long time. The Mount Shasta Light Publishing Company has books about Telos. If one can ascend to the fifth dimension of Telos, there are many waiting to 'show you around'!

*See Glossary: Telos books

Yes, there is much to do at Mount Shasta. Much more than one visit can handle. Margaret and I spent nearly one week here, and that is enough for this time. We will return.

But, I do have to tell you one more experience. Several times we have eaten at the Berryvale Grocery Store. Whoever heard of eating at a grocery store? Well, we had not, but we were pleasantly surprised and we returned several times to eat when we felt hungry.

We would stand in line in front of a counter with different types of cooked food, such as a variety of quiche, and when it was our turn to order, we would point to the food we wanted to eat. If it needed to be heated, it was heated immediately. Then we sat at a nearby table and ate. If we wanted a banana for dessert and it was sitting on a regular grocery store counter looking at us, waiting for us, we bought it.

Yes, Mount Shasta has been fun in more ways than one!

CHAPTER 5

MOUNT SHASTA JOURNEY

From Margaret:

August 7:

I am excited to return to Shasta. I consider it to be one of the most spiritual places in the country. I was there in 2012, but I did not see half enough. Today, the journey to Shasta is quick. First the airplane and then a rental car and Barbara and I are at the Alpine Lodge in the middle of Mount Shasta City. I settle into the hotel room and begin channeling to Telos, the community living beneath Mount Shasta. I am excited to do this because in 2012 it was delightful to channel with this vast community of higher dimension beneath Mt. Shasta.

* See Glossary for more on Telos.

I say hello to them and they answer immediately.

Hello, Margaret. We have been waiting a long time to see your return, to feel your presence 100% with us.

We see you first came in the door of music and then you came for the animals – the dolphins – and now you just walk in and sit down.

We welcome you. We love you. We cherish your work for the planet. Worlds are melding, merging. There will no longer be a dimensional separation.

Come fall asleep. Come to us. There is a celebration going on – the old Venus connection.

Your Telos Team.

August 8:

8-8-8 is a special day throughout the world because the repeating numbers are so rare. This combination creates great potential power when dimensions can be open and fluid.

Channeling from Adama, leader of Telos:

Margaret, what are your concerns here? What have you wanted to tell us?

I answer, dear Adama, I am concerned about the terrible fires in California, Oregon and Washington State. The trees are suffering. I have brought the Vortexes to bring healing because of the fires.

Adama: Yes, use these Vortexes to strengthen the trees to withstand this time of drought and fire.

Frequencies. You saw how the mass media and films can agitate and unnerve the people, keeping them unbalanced.

Frequencies. You know you are in the Telos Zone when you can speak quietly and deliberately and with humor and get your words, ideas across with ease and grace. Telos telephone.

The Trees are naturally tranquil. The humans need to be enough at peace to be able to link into tranquility. You come as a water being to pour love on the tree fire situation.

Here in Telos everyone speaks and everyone listens. The trees speak. The stones speak. The animals speak their wisdom. There is no fear here. All grow and thrive naturally with God's Grace. Our great halls are available through the heart intent of the individual. We are rejoicing in the gathering of the Brazilians and the French and all the people of the world here on this special day of 8-8-8 with Venus influence strong now raising the LOVE Creativity Healing Vibration.

Chasms need to be crossed. Tampering, tempering of the Spirit. Spirit heals. Love heals. Heart leads. Harmony abounds. It is very easy really.

Everyone wants the people on the planet to be peaceful. It will happen. The ego -- the I go -- focus needs to be diminished and blended into the frequency of the whole, each a shining, loving light. The fires affect you, me, and everyone, everything. The fires here, the fires of war, the fires of hatred, of judgment, of anger need to be tempered. Negativity cannot be met with negativity. It only begets more negativity.

Frequency. Change the Frequency to Love and Light. Then all things move forward. Mother Earth has moved on. To reach her you must be on a higher vibration. Yesterday, as you were coming here, you saw the land is powerful. There is fire beneath and fire on top. Humanity needs to focus on the environment -- all environments – the mind, speech, actions, attention, generosity, caring, compassion.

Come and join us below, above, within.

Our love to you from Adama of Telos.

This morning Barbara and I join Carmen's Brazilian group to go to Hedge Creek Falls, a place close by with tall trees. When the group heads down to the falls, I pause with Carmen and Barbara. The path is steep and one must walk carefully. When we come to a bench, we rest.

The trees are powerful and there are great clusters of boulders welcoming us as gatekeepers to the place. After a moment, I walk down the path a bit to speak to the trees and admire the moss-covered rock just beside the path. Above me is the morning sun.

Now I stop to kneel at a tree's roots where I begin to draw and speak the Vortexes. The trees know the Vortexes and welcome them. Earlier, in my mind's eye, special symbols appear that are related to this area, time and space. These are the Universal Law of Life and the Spiritual Law of Choice. Also, the Universal Law of Innocence, Truth and Family with the Spiritual Protection of the Family. When combined I see the symbols are echoing each other.

Then I see the symbol of Spiritual Freedom of Man, and I receive a message, *Life. All is Life. Family – we are all one. Freedom – freedom for all to live exuberantly and vibrantly.*

Now I join Barbara, and it is 12 noon, the most powerful moment of 8-8-8. We climb up the path and sit for a moment in a wooden gazebo to speak with an older man who is deeply spiritual. We talk about the world. He reminds us it is 8-8-8, the day of power, the day of Venus. Yes, we know. And we are happy we are sitting with such a spiritual man.

A few minutes later, Carmen comes with her group and announces that we are going to Panther Meadows on top of Mount Shasta. My heart leaps up! I've never visited and I want very much want to go to this spiritual place.

Soon we are driving up to the top of Mount Shasta. We pass the magnificent Kingdom of the Great Trees. They look wonderful!! I am crying with joy.

Further up, I see some tree damage and I learn later there has been an avalanche.

The mountain shows itself as we ascend higher and higher to the top. When we park near the top, we leave the van and sit together to admire with reverence the mountain, the essence, the warmness, the welcoming. A heart-shape cloud appears above us.

Now Carmen channels Saint Germain and we sit and listen as intense sunshine pours down on us and the mountain. We are totally connecting with the mountain. All is overwhelming in presence and beauty. At the tree line, I see small clusters of pinecones at the top of the trees, reminding me of clusters of little birds gathered.

In the evening we go the Angel Pageant and Youth Choir Concert held yearly, and the next day, August 9, we return to the same place to watch a performance of the Life of Jesus. Many are here, reliving the powerful event of the past. As we watch I see a lenticular cloud outline Mount Shasta. Then a heart-shaped cloud appears and a golden eagle flies overhead.

In the early afternoon, I go with Carmen's group to the Lower Falls of the McCloud River with its beautiful deep pool waterfall. We watch many swimmers and bathers. Around us are pine and cedar trees and I stand with little ones, gently stroking them, examining their new growth, admiring, blessing them. I say to each, may you grow tall and become a big wonderful tree full of beauty and perfection.

Above us, a heart-shared cloud welcomes us.

At 5:00 p.m. we get ready to go again to the top of Mount Shasta. I silently speak to Adama of Telos about our busy schedules, and he responds: *Not so underneath. Enjoy the trip to the top. We will enjoy the sunset together. Our love to everyone. Adama.*

When we begin driving up the mountain, we pass tall guardian trees. Then all the trees begin welcoming us as old friends along the way. They seem to come forward energetically to welcome us. We are totally heart connected. In our van are tears of joy to see the trees and mountain in all its splendor.

When we come to an area of devastation from an earlier avalanche, we see many little trees beginning to grow. This is an example of beautiful rejuvenation.

Near the top of the mountain where we park, we give many prayers. I feel the full loving presence of Mount Shasta. The sun seems to brighten as it sets. After prayers, I draw Vortexes for the mountain and the little patches of delicate blue, white, and violet wild flowers. It seems appropriate that the flowers should receive the Vortexes for they give such beauty to the mountain.

When returning down the mountain, a Great Sun Pillar shows itself against the dark sky of the setting sun. A Blessing! Two young deer stand by the road. One even comes onto the road and stops.

August 10:

5:45 a.m. I receive early morning channeling from Adama of Telos:

Frequency. Healing is ever present here through the Sacred Flames, through the Temples, through the life below the surface which is in total harmony with the mountain, with Mother Earth and with the cosmic systems.

Impatience is offset by patience. Slow your frequency to be in tune with your flowers. The flowers each sing their own song and display their wondrous colors, designs and sacred geometry. Mother Earth loves her flowers. The birds and humans delight in their being.

Crystals reflect and enhance light. Crystals heal. Crystal record. The Great Crystal, Shasta Mountain, is a tower of healing for the individual, the collective, the planet, the beyond into space. All things are compatible in the Shasta frequency. Integrated love, peace, harmony. People come and partake of all that is offered here in all the dimensions and realities. That is why you try so hard to comprehend the reality when your mind is not the receiver but your heart is.

Music, color, Light. How do you capture that? How do you hold that? By raising your frequencies – by dropping the heavy weight of questioning, pondering, spiraling into despair or confusion.

Light. You love swimming in the deepest water. You are lifted up by that. Light, it is the same. Relax and accept – swimming – moving into higher frequencies of Light. It is accessed by your love frequency, your wonder frequency.

Margaret, you came here with the dolphins to heal the trees. The trees hold the whale and dolphin songs. They are old allies. Note the dolphin energies are in the void spaces between the tree branches.

Accept All. Love All. Give Light. Forgive. Life is a sanding process, removing discordant emotions from one's internal being. When you come to this level and are in a quandary, relax, breathe and give and receive love. Knotted emotions untangle and smooth. All things will be resolved.

There are many tools, many allies here. The Angels, the Masters. All frequencies are open. That is why you saw the precious plays of the Angels and the Life of Jesus against the 'backdrop' of Shasta.

Shasta is the play. Christ, the messenger. And all messengers. Light in the eye. Light in the heart. That is the ticket to Telos.

Adama.

August 11:

Morning dawn calls with a pink and blue sky. Soft presence, loving Shasta Mountain. I worked last night in Telos with The Flame of Resurrection that has the golden lotus base and golden flames. I have so much to learn.

At 10:00 a.m. Barbara and I begin driving to Lake Siskiyou and then we have a disappointment. We find the lake is too difficult to approach. We see it at a distance and we turn around and head to Mount Shasta City Park. This holds a powerful site, the headwaters of the Sacramento River which flows hundreds of miles to the south. When we reach the park we look for the river source and do not see it until we stop and ask. Then we realize that only twenty feet from us is water coming out of the ground, the source we are looking for. We kneel at the foot and put our hands in the cold, sparkling water which will become a vast river. The place is sacred, surrounded by trees. Everything is pristine. A jewel. A gift of the mountain. A complete surprise. 11:11 a.m.

August 12:

Today we will go to Stewart Mineral Springs where I attended a conference in 2012. It is few miles from Mount Shasta City. The weather in 2012 was wet and rainy, but today it is the opposite, very dry, golden and crystalline clear. Earlier the sky was so shrouded with clouds, Mount Shasta was not visible expect for partially one day.

Now, in 2015, we can clearly see Mount Shasta every day. Rather than being wet, the land is either golden dry grass or deep green and lush. However, some fires have burned some sections of trees.

We drive up to large gates at Stewart Mineral Springs and then we drive down a deep gully over a bridge and up to a parking lot. Barbara and I return to the bridge by foot to send deep love to the clear, bright, pure water flowing over stones. We sound seven OMs to the water from both sides of the bridge.

Now I walk up to a beautiful covered bridge with water flowing below. A mountain jay is looking for old friends and food.

Before leaving Stewart Mineral Springs, Barbara promises the trees that nothing will happen to their land and they rustle in agreement.

Tonight there is a possibility of going up Mount Shasta to see a meteor shower. Should I go? I receive a channeled answer:

Did you go to find the meteor on the last trip (2012) at 3:00 a.m.? No. *This is an echo. The key is the deep connection to Shasta – the heart connection to the Guardian. This key is to open the information for you to know and recognize and to hold.*

I ask Mount Shasta: I have bought five obsidian stones, volcanic glass, for healing. Can you comment?

Answer*: Clarity, sharpness and cutting. Volcanic activity frozen in glass. Use for cleansing. Sharp removal of negativity. Fire and Air – release of steam (Water) becomes glass. A door that cannot be crossed. Protection. What was moving now stops and holds in clarity.*

This evening we enjoy an amazing concert at the foot of Mount Shasta by Anton Mizerak and Laura Berryhill, both excellent musicians. Their music is delicate and soothing and in perfect harmony with the mountain. During the concert, we do a meditation to travel within the mountain and I visualize going through green obsidian glass doors to reach the inside of the mountain.

*See Glossary: Shasta music.

August 13:

In the morning, Carmen broadcasts by SKYPE to Sao Paulo PAX TV. She invites us to speak and I speak about the love power of the Mount Shasta and about seeing the Milky Way Galaxy from near the top. From where I was standing I felt the immensity of the Galaxy and that I was a part of it.

*See Glossary: PAX TV.

Later in the day, we drive up Mount Shasta for a closing ceremony which Carmen performs yearly here. She channels Saint Germain about new happenings next year, more international cooperation, new beginnings.

August 14, the day we leave.

Margaret Channeling:

Dear Shasta Mountain, it is very hard to leave this place of peace and power and extreme beauty. There are so many dimensions here. Overhead, large space craft. Beneath the surface, the ancient and present-day of the Telos community.

Sacred Flames burn here beneath the surface. The Flame of Resurrection. The Flame of Healing. The Flame of Love. Mother Earth's heart is close to the surface here. The mountains were created by her internal fire. Take the Shasta Frequency and make it your own. Peace and Beauty, Love, Harmony and Healing.

So many gather here to drink the pure water, the pure love of the Mountain, distant yet close. Always present. An honor to be here. The doors are always open. Think on Shasta and you are here. The frequency influence of Shasta is world wide – planetary.

The basic frequency of Light (Life) is Love. Carry that through your life. That is the heart song of the humans. Love is the basic principle of creation. You saw the wonder of the Milky Way. That was my gift to you and to the group. Each one will receive more gifts as they give their gifts. Each one a fountain of Joy and Harmony and Love – Light – Peace. Peace, Love and Light.

Colors, moods, radiance. Radiate healing Love. It is all very simple. The animals, birds, and sea creatures do it naturally. Their instinct is to love, to create. Humanity is more complex. Their thoughts shade the expression of love. Sometimes it becomes lost or dim but it reignites again. It is always there, the core principle, LOVE.

Blessing from Shasta. We are always with you in peace and in love.

From Saint Germain of the Violet Flame:

You saw me in my light. You saw me as the little deer who stopped the van on the mountain.

Accept all. Love All. Work for the healing of the planet.

Thank you, dear Shasta, for your radiance and understanding.

Thank you, dear Saint Germain.

CHAPTER 6

NIAGARA FALLS

From Barbara:

August 28:

Last year we visited Niagara Falls, and now, this year, we are returning and we are excited to go. Before going, however, we speak about our upcoming journey via SKYPE to PAX TV of Brazil which will send our message to the world via television.

A year ago we specifically went to Niagara Falls to see a dragon considered by many to be the spirit guardian of the continent of North America. Was he there last year? Yes. Will he be there this year?

We also are expecting to attend a second EcoSpirit Native American Environmental Conference addressing the need to clean up Mother Earth's environment.

We do not live far from Niagara Falls. A little over an hour's drive. As we cruise along toward Niagara Falls, we love the beautiful weather being given to us. Not too hot and not too cold. The sun is lurking a bit behind light clouds, but there is no hint of rain.

Last year we took the 'back roads' to Niagara Falls, but this year we take the New York Thruway toward Buffalo. When we reach Exit 50, we turn off the mighty big road, and I, sitting beside Margaret who is driving, have in my hands maps showing which roads we should take.

Well, within five minutes, the map shows me a choice to turn left for a more direct way to reach Niagara Falls or right, the long way. I say to Margaret 'left' and Margaret says 'right'. She has not seen the map, but she is emphatic. And so, okay, we turn right. At first this takes us east and then it begins to gradually circle to the left to approach the airport. After the airport, we continue and continue and continue until we reach Expressway 190, the direct route to Niagara Falls.

We don't need Expressway 190 now! We are coming to the busy part of Niagara Falls city and we are soon arriving at the Sheraton At The Falls Hotel where we will be staying and where the conference is being held.

The staff here is very friendly and we are given an excellent room on the fourth floor where we rest for a time before returning to the front desk to ask for a taxi to the falls itself. We want to ride the Maid of the Mist boat. That is of uppermost importance just now.

A taxi is phoned and we are told to sit next to the front desk and wait for the driver to come for us.

And so we sit and wait. And wait and wait and wait. Where is the driver?! We know the last Maid of the Mist boat is 6 p.m. Our watches tell us it is just after 5 p.m. Will we be too late for the last boat?

A hotel bagman, who begins to realize our predicament, takes pity on us and tells us to follow him outside the hotel. He will personally find a taxi for us.

Yes! He does!

We jump aboard and the taxi man begins moving us smoothly along toward the boat ticket office. He is a friendly driver and as we are talking to him, I ask where is his homeland.

Pakistan.

Pakistan??????

Wow!

I tell him one of our books was translated into Urdu a few years ago, and we were personally escorted through Pakistan to speak about the book.

When we reach our destination to buy tickets to board the Maid of the Mist, he gives us his name card and tells us to cell phone him when we want to return to the hotel.

Yes. Of course. We like this Pakistani who is treating us as nicely as his comrades treated us in Pakistan.

And now, as we hurry through a park with many trees to reach the ticket office, we are still worried we will be too late for the last boat.

Well, no. Not at all. The line to buy tickets has less than ten people.

After buying our tickets, we take an elevator to stairs going down toward the boat. No one is rushing. We stop rushing.

We are given blue Maid of the Mist raincoats, and we begin putting them on as we walk closer to the boat that will take us. When we reach the boat, we stand in line to board and there are less than twenty people ahead of us. Wow!

We board and climb steep stairs to take a place at the railing where we had stood last year. Chinese tourists are taking places at the railing, too. They are very excited about the boat ride that will begin almost momentarily.

And yes, when the boat begins to move slowly, we are all very excited, especially when we reach the first falls. The water begins spraying mightily onto our raincoat hooded faces and we are all screaming with joy and happiness.

Interesting, both Margaret and I know the dragon is at the first falls, and we put our minds on him to greet him.

And now, just as we are at this first falls, the sun comes out mightily, and a rainbow, then two rainbows,,,, HUGE RAINBOWS,,,, enfold us, our boat, and the falls into ONE BIG DRAMATIC RAINBOW SHOW.

Wow!

Now I realize that the dragging of feet, from reaching the hotel to waiting a long time for a taxi to bring us to the Maid of the Mist has been a blessing in disguise! WE NEEDED TO BE HERE AT EXACTLY THIS MOMENT.

Thank you, whoever has helped with this 'miracle'.

The Chinese are clicking their cameras regardless of the mighty spray coming from the falls. I hope when they reach their homeland, some photographs will show the rainbows.

As the Maid of the Mist is slowly moving away from the first falls in order to reach the huge set of falls, I am thinking of last winter when the cold has frozen the falls. I am looking at them now and I can hardly believe they could completely freeze!

When we reach the big falls, the pilot pauses our boat and we sit for a time admiring the scenery. I think of the 'dare devils' who have walked across these falls on a suspended rope. Well, I know I will never be one of them!

As for the fascination of the falls, it is the POWER of the place that cannot escape the attention of all who come here.

And, I am thinking, this is the homeland of the dragon, guardian of North America.

We are at the center of the Niagara Escarpment that extends miles and miles and miles in all directions.

In the old days, 450 million years ago, maybe more, this was an ancient sea where billions of shellfish lived. When they died, their shells fell to the bottom of this ancient sea to mingle with other shells and rocks. Eventually, these shells and rocks grew in mass so that they extended high up and wide thousands and thousands of miles.

This was the time when Mother Earth was not experiencing negative energies, and so the Niagara Escarpment grew into a massive positive energy structure of shells and rocks. And, today the energy of the Niagara Escarpment is as positive and powerful as in earlier times.

How does one use this power? With the mind, one can overlay this powerful positive energy onto what needs to have better energy. Can you imagine how powerful this earth would be if everyone sent out masses of positive energy at the same time?

In any case, it is wonderful to be on the Maid of the Mist boat to experience the power of Niagara Falls. The mind begins to imagine PERFECTION for Mother Earth.

When we reach the boat landing and take off our blue Maid of the Mist raincoats, we return slowly to the green park with the intention of phoning our Pakistani cab driver. But then we decide to stay a few minutes at the park. Margaret will wander close to the river where it drops into the falls and I will sit on a park bench to watch the birds who have come here to scrounge for food.

I find a bench without other occupants, and I sit and begin watching the birds pecking here and there. I talk to them, say hello to them, admire their beauty.

I know they can hear me, read my mind, and I wait until they have decided I am not a threat. Then they begin to come toward the bench to peck for food. Finally some are at my feet strongly pecking.

I realize that we humans often are eating while we are sitting on park benches. Crumbs, tiny crumbs, drop to the pathway at our feet, and the birds know this. I am alone on a bench and they consider me no threat. Soon they are pecking for crumbs at my feet. I am amazed at how many tiny crumbs are at my feet!

Fun to watch this.

When Margaret returns from her walk at the river dropping into a falls, we go to the entrance of the park to make a phone call to our Pakistani cab driver. He answers and says he will arrive in about ten minutes.

As we are waiting, we watch a nearby old horse hitched to a buggy carrying a hefty woman waiting for tourists to climb aboard for a buggy ride. When we pet the old horse, we immediately realize he is not happy. He is old, yes. Is his body hurting? Maybe.

What can we do? Nothing to help him.

What can he do? Nothing. He does not speak.

A taxi arrives and stops and a white-turbaned driver gets out to ask if we are the two ladies waiting for a ride to the hotel.

Yes.

He says the taxi driver we are waiting for cannot come immediately and so he, the white-turbaned one, has been asked to come for us. Do we mind? No.

We climb aboard his taxi as he explains that the other man is his friend and they help each other when help is needed.

Interesting.

Here is a turbaned man from India who has joined with a man from Pakistan to do the work. Even more interesting, we soon learn this Sikh from India lives in the area where India and Pakistan meet. The land looks the same on both sides of the border. Governments make borders. As for this border, I am sure the people look the same no matter which side they live on, and friends are created regardless of the border.

Today has been an interesting day! We end it by having supper at a Thank God Its Friday restaurant attached to our hotel, and we can even have our supper bill charged to our hotel bill.

Cooperation. Another snippet of cooperation has come to us today.

More from Barbara:

August 29:

The conference begins at 8 a.m. this morning and we are happy it will be on the first floor of the hotel. We take the elevator from the fourth floor, location of our room, to the lobby, and then we walk beyond the front desk to enter a big room with many chairs. But, where are the conference folks? No one is here.

Just before entering the room, we pass a table with a seated woman who gives us a wristband for the conference. We return to her to ask where are the people and she has a surprising answer. The opening will be delayed two hours because Expressway 190 is undergoing big construction and thus there are huge lines of stalled cars waiting to reach their destination.

Oh Dear!!!!

And, another Oh Dear!!!!!

Yesterday we were supposed to take 190 to reach Niagara Falls city and we turned the opposite way. Well, thank you whoever 'Upstairs' has directed us to do this. Obviously, we were saved a long waiting time.

Well, the conference does begin, and to our surprise, Margaret and I are asked to say a few words before the assigned speakers begin. We are not ready but we must speak anyway. We know the conference is focusing on the need to clean up damage to Mother Earth, and we know plastic clogs the waterways, such as the Pacific Ocean that feeds tons and tons of fish, dolphins and whales. Last year Margaret and I were called by the whales to come to the Pacific and establish 'beacons of Light' up and down the Pacific North American coast. We speak about this, and we continue speaking by saying the public needs to pay attention to trees needlessly being cut down, especially because trees produce oxygen which we all need.

And yes, we speak about artificial food being fed to cattle to make them fat, and humans who eat this food becoming fat. Health problems develop, such as diabetes. Focus needs to be on cutting this type of 'fat' food and putting concentration on organic food.

One of the speakers tells about a pollution problem caused by a factory allowing poison used in manufacturing to drain out of the factory and into a nearby pond, home of many turtles and fish. By coincidence, I (Barbara) have just received an amazing message from the Cayman Islands where my family owns land. Dozens of turtle hatchlings had emerged overnight and gone into the sea to begin their lives.

The Niagara Falls speaker shows us an inexpensive hand-held test kit he uses to test the condition of water in this pond next to the factory. These test results are always below par. There is cancer evidence in the mouths of the fish and turtles living in this unsafe water cannot successfully breed. In shock, as I listen, I think of the little healthy turtle hatchings just born on a Cayman Island beach that will live a normal life. They have not received poison.

One conference speaker is Uqualla from the Grand Canyon tribe of Havasupai -- the people of the blue-green waters. His headdress resembles that of a bird and this headdress is WONDERFUL to see. We learn he comes from a family who has a Medicine Man Grandfather, and his mother taught him and his siblings the ancient ways of the tribe. I was surprised when he mentioned that his tribe lives so far from the entrance to the Grand Canyon, it can take four days walking to reach the entrance. As a child, he lived so far from the rest of the world, he did not see a 'foreigner' until he was, I think, eight years old. When he first saw a White Woman, he started to cry because he thought her mouth was bleeding. Then he learned she was wearing lipstick. In any case, Uqualla is now an adult, and has been an adult for a long time. He travels far and wide to give lectures and his lecture at Niagara Falls conference holds our full attention.

The next day, Sunday, August 30, finds us still in Niagara Falls and we are in a very special place -- in front of a statue of Nikola Tesla. In my room where I am writing you via my computer is a clock that gives me the time in bold red numbers. There is no a.m. or p.m., but I know whether it is morning or evening. Just now, the clock numbers are reminding me that it is time to think about breakfast.

Why do I have this clock in my computer room? It protects me from radiation coming from the computer. Nikola Tesla is behind this concept.

For nearly fifteen years, I wore a Tesla female-sized wristwatch and when it broke, I had to buy another. However, the watch-making company had stopped making female wristwatches and my only choice was to buy a male watch. This proved to be too big for my wrist and so I had to give up.

The big clock sitting about nine feet from my computer gives me protection in my room.

Who is Nikola Tesla, developer of this protection? An electrical and mechanical engineer born in Croatia who made his way to the United States to become involved in the field of wireless transmission of energy. If you want to learn more about him, check the Internet, and it will tell you that he wanted to light up the world by using the vibrating waves of the earth to generate unlimited power.

Yes, he experimented and he succeeded.

On Goat Island at Niagara Falls is a stature of Tesla. Margaret and I visit his statue, and we are proud to do this.

*See Glossary: Tesla.

Niagara Falls, you have provided us with experiences that we have enjoyed very much.

CHAPTER 7

NIAGARA FALLS

From Margaret:

August 29:

The sun is rising in the east. It is a brilliant day, the day of the full moon, called the Corn Moon by Native Americans, and I am thinking of Corn Woman, protector of the waters and all of Nature.

Yesterday here at Niagara Falls, Barbara and I went on the Maid of the Mist boat late in the afternoon. It was bright and beautiful with a clear sky. As soon as the boat moved close to the falls, an amazing rainbow appeared and then a second one. Double rainbows. They stayed with us the entire trip on the boat, and their rainbow colors were equally balanced, bright in clarity.

I saw the Dragon, Guardian of the North American Continent. He was bright, white, all colors in one. White in Love and Purity. Later, I ask him, dear Dragon of Niagara Falls, do you have a comment for us?

He responds: Margaret, I felt your presence, you and Barbara, your focus totally on me. The Sun was shining with all brightness. The energy was swirling as the boat, Maid of the Mist, moved up into the falls. I saw you scanning for my presence, for my energy, not realizing that you were in it immediately upon arrival in Niagara Falls.

The rock layers hold me. They are the gates to the falls. You came on an obscure route, not seeing the falls or the river which made the boat ride more impressive, more overwhelming.

Niagara Falls, the stage of power, shows the great power of Mother Earth. This is the true water show!

You are a water person and carry the love of the water. All the dolphins and whales are here, the water birds, the other sea creatures. They cheer the human beings seeing one point on Earth of true power.

The human is a guest and has no power compared to the immense power of the Elementals. This is true of all life. This understanding needs to be the basis of life going forward on the planet. Humanity needs to be in harmony with the natural world. There is no separation. Care for one is care for all. All systems are interrelated.

Care and kindness come first when dealing with all systems -- humans meeting humans, humans treating other humans, humans living on Earth -- not disturbing the planet but living in harmony with the planet.

Disregard for the planet's systems causes injury and malfunctioning. The rivers are clogged with algae. The fires burn in the West. The soil is depleted of nutrients. The air has lost its oxygen. Smog and storms have increased. Weather has become imbalanced. The tectonic plates have been affected. Shorelines lost, water rising, snow melting, glaciers disappearing. Last winter the dumping of 10 feet of snow in an early winter storm was here.

It is good the friends of Mother Earth are gathering. Let their information get out world wide. Their hearts are true, their minds fixed on finding solutions for the current problems.

Blessings to the people who gather and hold the mission of preserving the integrity of the Nature Systems.

Enjoy the time together. Work hard.

I am the Dragon of Niagara Falls, Guardian of the North American Continent.

Barbara and I are attending a conference at Niagara Falls on how to restore the environment. It is the Second Annual EcoSpirit Environmental Conference. It begins with everyone being pleasant, and yet each is thinking on a dedicated focused level about how to help the environment. We were surprised to be asked to speak first. I spoke about the channeling which I have just given you.

In the afternoon, when there is a break in the conference, Kim, a friend from Canada, walks with me to the falls to touch base with the power and focal point of this location, source of the power.

Blessings to the falls and to the Niagara Falls Dragon!

August 30:

This morning, 6:35 a.m. I am in the hotel room knowing I am sitting within the energy field of the falls. I am pulled to work with the Vortexes. I write them on my notepad to honor the Earth.

*See Glossary for Symbols of Vortexes.

I thank Mother Earth for this day. Each day is a new ticket for life on her planet. Thank you, Higher Worlds, for direction and oversight. Thank you, brothers and sisters for the gift of the Vortexes, the healing Symbols, high principles, guideposts, frequencies, fine tuning, attunement, ascension.

I begin reading, speaking and drawing the Vortexes, forwards and backwards, from the universal to the personal, from the personal to the universal.

The Universal Law of Movement and Balance comes forward for the water and the falls, and the Spiritual Law of Strength, Health and Happiness comes forward for the Dragon and for all living on Earth.

Yesterday, a thought question came to my mind while watching the river dancing to the falls. Are the water molecules hurt when they go over the falls? The answer came: *Are the water molecules hurt when they come down as rain?* No. As rain, water comes down as droplets of love and nutrients. When they come down frozen as snow, they come as hexagonal crystals. Both aspects are a blessing to the planet.

During another break in the conference, we go with Kim to Goat Island where we see a monument to Nikola Tesla. We also walk above the Cave of the Wind close to falling water. Amazing sights!

At the end of the day, the Dolphins speak to me about those who have attended the environmental conference:

Each person is a caretaker for the planet in his or her own way. Everyone's style and background is different but what unifies the group is the care and cherishing of the planet and the environment so that viable life on the planet will continue. Some speak with soft voices. Some speak straight on the facts and historic legacy. Much is given to think about.

Now I am again thinking of the Niagara Falls Dragon and he speaks:

I, the Dragon, Guardian of the North American Continent, was present and for you, I could be felt at the water's edge.

The glory of the falls overwhelmed all visitors and they went away changed. Interactions between national groups were smooth and cordial. All the visitors to this place must walk softly and with respect. The power present diminishes the ego and a great reverence of the spirit blooms.

Here is water power, expansion -- constantly flowing, moving, dancing, crashing below in a great waterfall of water. This great vortex of power sweeps everyone up and tosses them over the falls to begin again, changed with the wonder of the splendor of it all.

The trees, the wildflowers hang on the edge. The people, too, holding onto the edge. Water, time, life moves forward quickly. Everyone saying a prayer of gratitude and awe.

Vast power, power generator. Great ideas have come from here. Great accomplishments are celebrated. Many diverse people are swept into the Vortex of Change. Nothing will be the same again.

Closeness and vastness, change accomplished, Mother Earth is heard and felt today in everyone's heart.

Heart resonance, not head. Heart! The Power of the Falls!!! I am there with that Power. Rest one more night in my domain.

The Niagara Falls Dragon, Spirit Guardian of the North American Continent.

CHAPTER 8

POPE FRANCIS COMES TO U.S.A.

J oint Journals:

First from Barbara:

September 22, the day before the Equinox when all should be equal, Pope Francis of the Vatican begins his first visit to the U.S.A. Margaret and I have specifically gone to Washington, D.C. to be there when the Pope arrives. Thousands, probably millions, are watching this arrival moment.

Why is his arrival important? He has come to bring a message of peace and the importance of cooperation among all humanity regardless of wealth or position or poverty. He will be showing examples of the concept of everyone being equal.

We watch his first appearance at the airport of him climbing down the plane stairs, his right hand touching the railing. I am thinking he is a bit unsteady. Does he have a leg or back problem?

And then a wind comes up and his white clothes are ruffled enough to make his wide collar lift to whisk off the white cap perched on the back of his head. An attendant climbing down the stairs behind him grabs the white cap and it is back on the Pope's head before he reaches the tarmac to grasp the hand of President Obama who has come to greet him. They begin a hearty handshake, and I am thinking maybe the two have not met each other until now, but both have a similar opinion. They like each other. Smiles are on their faces and I can see they are speaking to each other in a friendly manner. Michelle Obama and the two Obama daughters stand by and watch.

And so, the U.S.A. visit of the Pope begins.

But here comes a surprise. A black, tiny Fiat car is brought up and the Pope climbs into the back seat. Directly ahead and behind the tiny Fiat are big, black vehicles one would expect to be used to transport the Pope. But no, he prefers the tiny Fiat. I think he wishes to be a simple man even though he is wearing the garb of the high priest of the Vatican.

And thus, we begin hearing comments of the Pope's preference for being like common people rather than looking like the 'Almighty'.

It is now close to the end of the afternoon of September 22, and Margaret and I have also just arrived in Washington. Our day begins with a 3:30 a.m. wakeup call from Joan the taxi driver who will take us to the train station for an early morning departure to New York and then a transfer to Washington D.C.

At the train station, we are surprised that few are waiting for the early train. Our thought has been that many will be going to Washington via New York City to see the Pope, and so, seats could be sold out. We wanted to leave early to avoid a possible seat problem.

Well, there is no seat problem. The train is nearly empty, and even though we stop nearly ten times to pick up passengers before reaching New York City, the train does not become full. Is everyone waiting for later trains? Will these be full?

When we reach Penn Station in New York City, there are many passengers waiting to board trains. We hire a 'red cap' porter to take us to our train destined for Washington, and he puts us aboard before the others. And yes, this train becomes full. Even overfull. All seats are sold out and passengers are asked to take later trains.

When our train for Washington begins movement, we sit comfortably and watch out the window as we travel across the land. We stop several times, but when the stop for Baltimore is announced, we know Washington is just ahead with only one more quick stop at New Carrollton.

Union Station in Washington has many walking here and there with big suitcases, and now our attention is on hailing a cab to take us to the Capitol Skyline Hotel. Will there be any cabs available? We know Washington will be stuffed with people coming to see the Pope.

Well, we have no problem finding a cab, and within minutes we are driven to our hotel. Earlier, when we booked a room by phone, Margaret spoke with the manager who said she would reserve a room for us with a view of the Capitol Building. Sure enough, when we enter the room, the Capitol Building is looking at us through the window!

September 23:

The world press is covering the morning event of Pope Francis meeting President Obama at the White House. Of course the roads to the White House are packed with people wanting to glimpse the Pope as he is being driven in his tiny black Fiat. When he does arrive, there is an outdoor formal greeting ceremony for honored guests on the South Lawn. An estimated 20,000 are gathered to watch. I am surprised that the ceremony includes red-coated males performing in the manner of British soldiers of ancient times.

When the formal greeting ceremony is over, the Pope and the President stand on an outdoor stage to speak. The Pope speaks in English, a language he is unaccustomed to using, but he is easy to understand. He begins by saying he is the son of an immigrant family and he has come to the United States for the first time with a desire to learn many things and to share his experiences.

President Obama listens carefully to every word and I am thinking that the Pope has appropriately chosen the subject matter of immigration to begin his speech. The U.S. government is just now tangled in an immigration dilemma. Many want no more immigration and the subject of deportation comes up often.

Pope Francis' family emigrated from Italy to Argentina, and he is the first Pope to be born in South America. His U.S. visit begins after he has stayed a short time in Cuba which is also a 'hot' topic. Efforts just now are being made to begin normalizing a relationship between the two countries that has been 'bottled up' for fifty years. While in Cuba, the Pope even met with Fidel Castro, who figures heavily in the 'bottled up' relationship.

On the South Lawn of the White House, Pope Francis also speaks about the need to pay strong attention to climate change which is impacting the environment and causing destruction. He tells us the poor are affected by this destruction, and as the Pope is speaking, many hearing him are clapping approval of his words.

When the Pope and the President finish their speeches, they turn and enter the White House for a private conversation. Then, after he leaves, the Pope performs a midday prayer at a cathedral. In the afternoon, he goes to the Basilica of the National Shrine of the Immaculate Conception, which I call Mother Mary's cathedral. It is easily reached via the metro running through Washington, but today I know thousands will be going there to try to glimpse the Pope. And so, it is better to remain in Washington and let the others struggle while Margaret and I watch on television. Yes, television has a great advantage just now.

September 24:

Today we leave Washington to arrive in New York City for the Pope's visit there. We leisurely check out of the Capitol Skyline Hotel before noon, and we are soon on the train heading for New York City. We arrive at Penn Station midafternoon and our hotel is across the street from the station. It will take less than five minutes to wheel our bags to the hotel. This is not the best of hotels, but it has the advantage of being across the street from Madison Square Garden, destination of the Pope's event tomorrow night.

He will be very busy while in New York. Tomorrow morning, 8:30 a.m., he will be speaking to the United Nations General Assembly, and then he goes to the site of the World Trade Towers that were brought down September 11, 2001. At 4 p.m. he will be in East Harlem visiting a school that has many poor children.

We know the Pope has a special place in his heart for children. In Washington, we watch Pope Francis riding in his popemobile rather than the tiny Fiat when a security man suddenly picks up a small child and rushes the child to the popemobile for the Pope to kiss her. The Pope loves kissing babies and blessing the sick. Every gesture from him is done with a smile on his face and cheers from the crowds.

When the Pope finishes kissing the small child, the security man returns the child to her mother. Yes! This is wonderful to watch. And it is wonderful to watch as the Pope suddenly descends from the popemobile to walk to the crowds cheering him along the roadway. I will never forget the drama of the Pope and the people and the people will not forget either.

Here is an interesting sideline. Pope Francis arrives in the U.S.A. just before the beginning of a full moon total lunar eclipse. It is said that this is a moment when linear time stops and energy floods onto the earth. One can program this incoming energy to help the earth. We cannot look out the window to see an effect, but there is an effect anyway.

I programmed the powerful, incoming energy with the thought of Peace. This is a prolonged lunar eclipse, five and one half hours, and I specifically programmed peace energies for our world during this entire time period.

What is interesting to me is that this past week, via TV, Internet, etc., millions throughout the world watch the Pope's visit. As mentioned earlier, he continually gives a message of peace and cooperation among all humanity regardless of wealth or position or poverty. He wants to show an example of everyone being equal. And so, when the eclipse arrives with its powerful incoming energy, millions are thinking about this man and his passion of peace and love.

I want to relate here to you that in my opinion Pope Francis fits into the concept of the one-hundredth monkey effect. One monkey learned how to wash a sweet potato in a new way. Other monkeys watched him and some began copying his new technique. Then others copied, and others, and when the one-hundredth monkey learned the new technique, all monkeys did the same. I think Pope Francis is giving us an example of this.

More eclipses are coming, and we will have a repeat of this September eclipse. Time will stand still as energy floods in. My thought is that if great numbers are determined to think peace at the moment of an eclipse, our world would have a better chance of adopting peace. That is what we all want.

From Margaret:

September 23, Equinox Morning in Washington, D.C.:

Both Barbara and I have an interest in the Pope coming to the U.S.A. during the Equinox and Eclipse. We will see the Pope in Washington, DC, capital of the nation, at the moment of the Equinox, a time when the sun rises over the earth's equator and thus night and day approximately are equal throughout the earth. This occurs in the fall as well as in the spring.

I awaken early at 3:22 a.m. in time for the exact moment of the Equinox at 4:20 a.m. in Washington, D.C. I focus on Mother Earth and I know she is in perfect balance, straight up. Her relationship to the sun is equal sunlight in the north and equal sunlight in the south. The sun's rays are directly on the Earth's Equator and the day and the night are equally balanced.

I know the sun will rise directly over the Capitol Building today. I think the early planners for Washington, D.C. knew the significance of placing the Capitol Building in a relationship to the rising of the Equinox sun for balance. A few years ago, when I attended a Native American sunrise ceremony at a prayer vigil for the earth near the Washington Monument, I saw that the sun rose over the Capitol at the time of the Equinox.

Do you know the significant buildings on the Mall are in alignment as a cross? On one axis is the Capitol Building, the Washington Monument is in the middle, and then the Lincoln Memorial. On the other axis is the White House, the Washington Monument in the middle, and then the Jefferson Memorial. All receive the early rays of the Equinox sun.

For me, the feeling of the early morning is peaceful. In meditation, I connect to Mother Earth and the power of her movement, tilting and re-tilting forward and backward for the changing of the seasons in her two hemispheres. Today is fall in the North and spring in the South. How impressive. All of life as we know it depends on these movements.

Washington is awake now, focusing on the visit of the Pope. His activities begin at the White House, then a parade around the area of Constitution Avenue with the Washington Monument in the background, and finally he goes to Mary's Church. We are in the energy field of all this. Pope Francis is sending his message of peace and love and we are sending our message of peace and love. We see the people responding to him with peace and love.

The country feels uplifted and this is happening when the full moon Lunar Eclipse is ready to occur. After the Pope leaves, I receive channeling from the Higher Worlds. Specifically, most of it has to do with the importance of the eclipse.

The door is opened to receive and to connect to All That Is. The heart of Mother Earth stands open as the dance of the earth, sun and moon eclipse brings high codings and activation to life forms on earth.

The large sun is full of love and the universe is abundantly pouring knowledge, understandings, harmonies onto the earth. Dimensions merge. Time stops and the breath is held to begin again. Love and compassion is life. Life is love and compassion. That is growth of the Spirit.

Flowers hold their secrets and sacred geometries and release their understanding at the time of the eclipse. Water holds Light and feels the movement of the moon pulling, drawing, activating the vitality of the water. Liquid magma moves. The earth is expanding. The sun gives love to life-building ingredients. The moon puts them in motion.

Motion is life enhancement — movement and balance, strength, health and happiness — expanding one's consciousness in every direction. This happens at the moment of the eclipse. In the eclipse shadow comes revelation. In revelation comes joy.

The earth wishes to share these secrets. Her heart is very close to connect to. Her generosity to support life is unceasing and can be witnessed, acknowledged with gratitude at this time of the eclipse. Music is in the air. Songs of love can be written. The body's cells sing these songs. Let the songs come to the surface for the mind to comprehend.

Nuances, subtleties — everything is alive. Capture the fleeting understandings of Nature — the bird's feathers in the wings and tail, the patterns of the fish that augment movements, the dance of the trees, the waving of the branches, the complexities and poetry of wild flowers and cultured flowers, patterns of snowflakes, designs on water, movement of wind creating patterns. Delights. During an eclipse there are subtle delights, often lost in the bright sun's presence, that rise to the surface.

The sun loves the earth and the moon and gives them love energy. The planets of the universe open up and share their gifts during the time of the eclipse during the disappearance of the moon, time stopping.

It is the time of celebration, to relax and receive. It is a fitting ending to the travels of a humble man, the Pope, who carries the fire of love and compassion. May humanity carry this fire that will light the world. It is all very simple and very complex.

Settle in as the eclipse continues and the effects continue afterward. Rest in the moment of movement and the opening of understanding. This is an emotional and cellular tune up. A growing and an expanding.

With love from the Higher Worlds.

Later, when I return home, after the Equinox and after the full moon lunar Eclipse, I ask the Dolphins and the Whales about the Love energy that has poured in during the Pope's visit. I say, we share the water element, the basic principle of life. The surface of the planet is at least 80% water. Our bodies are at least 80% water. Can you comment?

The Dolphins and Whales answer: Dear Margaret, you are at home in the oceans. You are at home with us. That is why you walk the beaches early in the morning to greet us. Humans and Dolphins and Whales hold the same heart energy field. We send out love frequencies through our codings, our breaching (whales), leaping (dolphins), spouting (whales), smiling (dolphins). We hold the integrity of the planet together, to balance the natural systems. That is why the Universal Law of Movement and Balance was given to us as being the Guardian according to universal understanding.

The Key is awareness – motion, emotion – action, reaction. Life participation is a gift to be cherished. The oceans, the land, the air need to be honored as the most precious treasure on earth. They are freely given to all to be cared for. Come into this awareness and all the busy-ness dies away. Every element is cherished and replenished.

It is love that moves the systems. Love, Joy, Celebration of Life. That is why the people flock to see the Pope to be in his energy field. For a moment, cities lift up – not stuck in the dreariness of commerce and political unawareness.

Mother Earth is a vibrant planet. Humans are tiny in form but great irritants if unaware and doing damage to the natural systems. We ask for awareness. We ask for love to be shared with all systems – grace and honor – awareness, moderation – sharing life on the planet.

We send out Light, our song. We balance the waters and the (tectonic) plates. Have the humans do the same. We are on this planet at the same time. You are on land and we are in the sea.

Mother Earth is a jewel Star to be foremost in everyone's thoughts and appreciations. Wake up and breathe. Cherish every moment here.

With love, your older Brothers and Sisters, the Whales and Dolphins of the Oceans.

Earth is a water planet. Cherish it.

Now PAX TV of Brazil asks Barbara and me to speak about Saint Francis of Assisi who lived centuries ago. On October 4, Brazil will have a big celebration for him.

I ponder what to say. What is the significance of the two Francis? I know both men hold great LOVE Energy.

I have seen children flock to today's Pope Francis to receive a kiss and a blessing in the same way as birds flocked to Saint Francis of Assisi to receive his words and blessings. LOVE has attracted the children and the birds. It is our lesson to learn to walk humbly, reaching out with our hearts to the children, to all people, to all of Nature. There are nearly 800 years in between 1220 and 2015 and yet the Love energy is the same.

I research the Internet for music played in Saint Francis' time and later, and I find joy.

I ask Emma to channel about the music.

Answer: you have found your soul's music. It has been waiting for you. From the past to bring forward to the now. The music dances forth in space. All of Nature loves this music.

The door to Ascension -- each of you is given a Key. You unlock the frequencies through music. Hold to the joy. It will never let you down. The high notes, the joyful notes, the dancing stream. Let there be light. Streams travel and never cease. Rejoice in the wonder of life, unceasing.

Emma

*See Glossary: Emma Kunz.

From Barbara:

I have been asked to speak on Brazil TV about a Francis who lived centuries ago in Assisi, Italy. His name eventually became Saint

Francis. For the people he was a miracle man, and he was a healer and a lover of Nature, especially birds.

Because my name is Wolf, I decide to speak about a wolf and St. Francis. Near his town of Assisi was a village of shepherds who peacefully tended their flocks of goats and sheep. Then one day a wolf killed and ate a member of the flock. This killing became a habit and the shepherds needed to stop the killing.

Three men armed themselves to kill the wolf and when he appeared, they attacked him. However, the wolf was strong and overpowered the men. He killed two and wounded the other, abandoning him. When news of the episode reached the villagers, they were horrified and extremely fearful that the wolf would eventually kill all of them.

Now the villagers decided to call in Saint Francis who was already a legend among the people. Surely, he would know how to dispose of the wolf, although they were fearful that the powerful wolf would also kill him.

When Saint Francis was summoned, he came immediately to help. The villagers locked themselves in the village while Saint Francis walked outside the premises ready to encounter the wolf. And yes, soon the wolf appeared and began circling St. Francis.

Saint Francis sat down and closed his eyes to meditate. Then he and the wolf connected mentally and Saint Francis asked the wolf why he was killing the villagers.

The wolf answered that he had become injured and his pack abandoned him because he could not keep up. He needed to eat to survive. He needed to kill the shepherds' flock. When the shepherds came after him, he needed to defend himself. He killed two and injured the third, which he abandoned because he did not want to eat the man.

Saint Francis listened to this information and began meditating for a solution. After a long time, he asked the wolf if he would stop the killing if the villagers agreed to feed him. Yes, the wolf promised. He would do no more killings.

Saint Francis and the wolf went together to the village to tell the people. As they entered, the villagers had much fear until Saint Francis told them that if they agreed to feed the wolf, he would not kill. The villagers immediately agreed and the first villager to feed the wolf was a close relative of one of the men who had been killed.

Brother Wolf, they started calling him, and he became great friends with all of them.

CHAPTER 9

BUFFALO, HORSES, BIRDS

BUFFALO

Joint Journals:

First from Barbara:

The buffalo have been living as a family on Mother Earth a long time. They live in peace with each other, and they respect other families living on this planet, including humanity.

When I was a child, my family lived in the eastern part of the United States, and one year during the summer we traveled West to see the Great Plains, the cattle ranches, the antelope, and yes, we traveled to see the buffalo.

One day, as we were traveling in a remote area with little population, we saw close to the road about twenty buffalo standing behind a wire fence. We immediately stopped the car and ran to the fence to see them. It was exciting for me because I had never seen a buffalo.

They had little tails and some had small horns. I saw that the front of the buffalo is bigger and wider than its back. Yes, I was full of curiosity about these wild creatures who lived in the western part of the continent!

Later, when I returned home, I had a thought. The wire fence blocking the buffalo from the road was too thin to keep them away from the road. They could have broken the fence if it had been their desire. I asked a Native American why the buffalo would tolerate the fence put up by humans and I was given an interesting answer.

They agreed to tolerate the fence because they agreed to respect what humanity wants. Peace is a prime desire for them. Peace among themselves and for all that live on Mother Earth, including humans who function with both negative and positive energies.

It was many years before I again saw buffalo. We learned from a friend who lived in an area of apple tree farms and other fruit farms that buffalo were living in this area. In particular, one farm had many buffalo allowed to live and roam on the farm without being harmed. In fact, no one in the area tried to hurt the buffalo.

One day our friend drove us to this area, and when we came close to the farm that had many buffalo, we saw them sitting in the shade of big trees. There were about seventy.

Before coming here, I had sent out a mental message to these buffalo asking that one would be close enough to us when we drive by.

Well, all the buffalo were sitting peacefully in the shade, and they were at least one or two hundred yards from the road. This was disappointing. We stopped the car and looked at them far away. Suddenly, a female buffalo stood and started coming toward us. Yes, I said to myself! She has received my mental message. She is coming toward us. Then a small buffalo rose and started walking behind the female. She quickened her pace, and her little offspring quickened his!

WONDERFUL.

However, a wooden structure was behind the farm buildings and the buffalo could not reach us.

Disappointment.

Well, it is now several months later and yesterday Margaret and I decide to return to see the buffalo. I do not put out a mental message to alert them. We go in the morning and within 1 1/2 hours we are at the farm, but at a different place because we take a different road. And, guess what. We arrive exactly beside a wire fence and within five feet are seven male buffalo looking at us. We stop the car and get out to greet them!

HELLO, FRIENDS, WE LOVE YOU!!!!

Just now Mother Earth has received powerful energy from the cosmos, and she will be receiving more in November. Since everything has a consciousness, including the buffalo, that night, after we leave the buffalo, Margaret channels them asking about the powerful, incoming energy. Here is their answer.

From Margaret:

Dear Buffalo, so many energies and codings are coming to Earth to help raise the consciousness of the humans. How are these energies affecting you and your group and how are you affecting your human neighbors and land and the larger environment?

Buffalo answer: Our essence is to be in our solidity. We reflect Mother Earth's thoughts and feelings during times of peace and the times of agitation. We relate to each other in a herd. The humans fragment into thought groups and activities. Some drive by unconscious. Some come bringing bouquets of love to our group or cluster.

We exist and hold the space for the animals. We used to be plentiful and now we are scarce. We cannot roam freely. We bring peace to the land and peace to the neighbors, the humans, animals, birds. We hold the stabilizing influence. We are solid on the land in our presence. Cease the rushing, the search. You are already where you are to be to anchor the codings coming in. Take our settle-ness into your being. Then you will not be buffeted by the winds of change. Settle into your being-ness. Connect deeply to the planet.

We moderate the raw energies by our presence. Come sit with us on the hill. We are an ashram of peace, energy field. That is why you have our picture with the deity of Arunachala and the stone from Arunachala, the place that has not moved. You cannot go to Arunachala today, this week, but you can come and visit us.

We are the Guardians of the Spiritual Law of Protection of Family.

The Buffalo.

Here is a P.S. The buffalo mention Arunachala, India, because it is noted as being one of the most stable places in the world. We wanted to enter this stable energy to spread it out to the world, but we could not go. There was too much to do.

On the day we drive to see the buffalo, we leave about 9:00 a.m. The day is bright and we have plenty of time. Barbara is sitting beside me as I drive, and she has triple road maps in her hands. As we go along, we check them. When we reach the farmhouse where there are the buffalo, we first see bales of hay and then the buffalo. They are close to the road behind a fence. Males. Big males.

We stop the car, go to the fence, and quietly send our love greetings to the buffalo, thanking them for their being. They are grazing. One looks at us but keeps eating. All are calm. We are pleased. In the sky above them are seven cloud formations. We know our cosmic brothers and sisters are here with us. We stay with the buffalo, loving to be with them, and then we quietly return to our car to drive to our friend's house. When we tell her we have seen the buffalo, she is pleased.

The day is not over for wonderful events. In the late afternoon I see lenticular clouds. I know these are special cloud formations and they remind me of Mount Fuji and Mount Shasta. In another direction, I see a cloud representation of the serpent of Serpent Mound in Ohio, a powerful energy point under the influence of the star cluster called Draco which has meteor showers now in October. The coil of the serpent is at one end and the undulating movement of the body extends to a long neck and mouth holding an egg form. This is amazing because I had forgotten that the serpent may have an egg in its month.

I know that many meteor showers are expected to come in November with codings to assist Mother Earth and humanity to advance. Are the October Draco meteors showers a part of this?

I channel for an answer:

Response: This has always been our timing. We are the forerunners for what is to come. We are shrouded in mystery but we bring high energies to the planet to spark creativity — advanced forms of energies to be used for the good — the welfare, the well being of the planet — to enliven the natural life systems.

From Barbara:

We are beginning to realize that we need to try to help balance energies in the world before the powerful November meteors come. These are peace and love meteors, positive energy, and so we want our top peace and love energy places to be in good shape, clean of negativity. We meditate on these energy places -- Serpent Mound, Cahokia, Mound Bottom, Toltec Mound, Etowah Indian Mound, etc.

When we are satisfied, we return to our concentration on animals, part of the energy system of Mother Earth. From the buffalo, we turn to the horse.

HORSE

From Barbara:

Internet examination has opened us to the EquiCenter, a therapeutic riding facility we can reach by a short drive. This place treats autistic children, other needy children, veterans with trauma, etc. We have a friend in Colorado, Annette Price, who also concentrates on healing with horses.

Can you imagine what this world would be like when many realize that horses are true healers? Maybe we will begin saying, "Good morning, Dr. Horse, I have a sore throat today. What do you recommend?" Actually we would not have to speak. The horse is a mind reader. He can aid us without words.

We phone the EquiCenter office to say we would like to visit to learn how the horse and the human can interact to bring a positive change to the human. Yes, please come, we are told with enthusiasm! All will be explained. Therapy sessions are between 3:00 p.m. and 8:00 p.m.

And so we are soon on our way to the EquiCenter at Honeoye Falls, located close to Mendon Ponds Park, which, to us, is a sacred place on the Niagara Escarpment. As explained earlier, the Niagara Escarpment began at least 450 million years ago when the area was a sea where billions of shell creatures lived. When they died, their solid shells clung to rocks and other structures to be part of a solid mass. Eventually, the buildup was enormous and it still remains to this day.

What is of interest to me is that this natural constructing of the Niagara Escarpment occurred when Mother Earth was experiencing no negative energy. To this day, the buildup remains positive. With this in mind, we travel to the EquiCenter knowing it is located within a positive area of energy.

Our journey by car is smooth, and in a very short time we are on Rush Mendon Road looking up at an extensive white-fenced area which we know is a paddock for horses. But,,,,, this paddock is VERY EXTENSIVE.

How many horses are at the EquiCenter?

When we speak with the head woman of this astonishing place, we learn that accepted horses will stay here 'forever'. Out of one hundred tested for therapy work, about seventy-five are turned away and twenty-five are accepted.

There is a reason for turning away so many. The horses must accept the condition of all patients coming here. There can be no impatience. Some patients will come with cerebral palsy, Down's syndrome, spinal injuries, visual impairment, mental and emotional problems. And recently, the EquiCenter is beginning to treat military veterans with mental disorders.

We sit at the end of an interior arena to watch the first child for the day come to be treated. She is with her mother, and we learn that the child's life is seriously restricted except when she comes for her horse therapy. We see she is smiling and smiling, knowing she is ready for royal treatment from the horse assigned to her and from three attendants who will be beside her as she is on the horse.

We learn that one child could not sit up when she first started horse therapy. Now she does sit up and when she is on the back of the horse, she is not only sitting up, but she is, when instructed, told to turn around and ride with her back to the horse's mane. She is also told to stand on the horse and to put her arms straight up. The child does this spontaneously and with no fear as the horse is steadily walking in the arena.

This is fascinating to watch!

The lessons are a half hour and then another child is given half-hour therapeutic instructions. One boy who looks to be about thirteen sits easily as he is put on the horse's back. My impression is that he is a natural horse rider. We are told he has only come to the EquiCenter for just over three months.

One of the children does not begin his riding lesson, as we had expected, but instead, he is taken from the arena. We are told that he is learning to groom his horse and even to clean the hoofs of the horse. Everything concerning the grooming of a horse will be shown to the boy, and this will be giving a calming, relaxing motion to the boy's body.

When Margaret and I attend these wonderful afternoon therapeutic sessions, we realize the importance of the horse in the world of humanity, and especially in the world of medical treatment. Are horses everywhere waiting to be asked to help with medical treatment?

From Margaret:

For me to visit the EquiCenter is like being given gifts of joy to witness the horse as healer and ally of the human.

As a Gift of Healing, I see the horse as a natural healer, observer, transmuter of human body frailties and the human emotional mind. The horse is patient, attentive and focused when on the same wavelength as the human rider and volunteer helpers.

We receive the Gift of Beauty at the EquiCenter because it feels as if we are in a bit of heaven. All is positive. All is in order. All is beautiful – the horse, the rider, the helpers, the arena, the environment.

The Gift of Welcome is given to us by the staff who welcomes us and allows us to observe amazing healing by horses and attendants making the children with special needs shine riding the animal of great power, size and strength. To them, sitting on a horse and riding is like sitting on top of the world. Joy bubbles up with the accomplishment of riding, staying on the back of a trotting horse, holding the reigns, keeping the balance, holding one's head high, the body centered and in rhythm with the horse.

I am given the Gift of Joy by seeing the expressions of the children, the parents, and the attendants when each assigned exercise is accomplished with relish and enthusiasm.

The Gift of Generosity is given by the volunteers who attend the riding children by holding carefully onto them, encouraging them, cheering them on to hold their hands high or outstretched or riding backwards. All amazing feats.

The Gift of Time and Place is given by this outstanding facility which is available for children with special needs, at risk youth, and wounded veterans and their families.

I see the Gift of Careful Planning and Management by the staff where a specific saddle goes with each horse, each bridle fits, and each child has his attention details met as to the size of a horse, nature of a horse, and the child's likes and dislikes. Included are schedules of riders, schedules of volunteers, schedules of horses, tack, feeding, watering, grooming, care. Because of careful planning and management, joy is here at the EquiCenter.

I see the Gift of Growth and Development given to a child who could not walk until she learned to ride a horse. That taught her body how it feels to walk.

I see the Gift of Being There in Strength and Beauty and Love which the horse gives to the special needs rider.

The Greatest Gift for the children is the erasing of disabilities with the accomplishment of riding and a rebirth of an ancient association of horse and rider. This is a proud heritage. They are old allies. Today the horse is nurturing the young so the young can reach a high goal. This brings joy to everyone.

In conclusion, we thank the EquiCenter staff for our amazing visit to a little bit of heaven on earth where miracles happen because of the horse. We have enjoyed this day of gifts!

BIRDS

From Barbara:

October 23:

Yesterday we spoke via SKYPE to Brazil's PAXTV about healing horses, and today we have thoughts about next week speaking about the birds. But first we need to visit the bird kingdom.

A few years ago we were with a group listening to a bird-man explaining about the owl he was holding on his arm. A screech owl. Well, the owl was not screeching and he was very still, not moving a muscle. The bird-man said the owl was blind. I knew he was not deaf. He was quietly listening to every word the bird-man was saying.

Birds are telepathic. Maybe the blind owl did not know every word his handler was saying, but he knew we listeners were hearing about the love and care of birds.

It was amusing when the man told us what happens when he would be taking his birds home after giving a lecture. Even before he arrived home, the birds knew when they were only few minutes away from arriving. The ones at home knew also, and they became excited. We knew he had extensive housing for them. Wouldn't it be fun if we could visit them now?

A phone call to his home receives no answer. What are we to do now?

A search of the Internet for other bird handlers alerts us to Wild Wings, a sanctuary in Mendon Ponds Park. Amazing! Of all the places on this planet where a sanctuary could be located, there is one no more than two miles from the healing horse center we have just visited.

We phone and we are told that visiting hours are between 10 a.m. and 2 p.m. every day except Wednesday and Thursday. Well, today is Friday, and within minutes we are in the car and driving to Wild Wings!

This place takes care of permanently injured 'raptors', birds of prey who, if remaining in the wild, would not survive because they could not hunt for food.

When we arrive and open the main office door, we are confronted by a busload of school children ready to visit birds in their individual enclosures outside the main office. A bird woman, owl in hand, is explaining to the children what they are about to see. By the way, Wild Wings is an educational facility for school children and everyone else.

This is perfect for us! We follow the group outside and we begin passing individual bird enclosures that are just now receiving a bit of bright sunshine. And yes, the birds are sunning themselves.

Margaret and I linger, stopping at every enclosure, saying hello to each bird. Soon the school children and their bird leader are several yards ahead of us.

Now we are hearing a hoot hoot from a barred owl, and I respond with my hoot hoot. The owl hoots again and I answer. Then again and again and again. What fun!

I ask Margaret to use her cell phone to reach our Native American friend in Missouri, and when the connection is made, I hoot to the owl and the owl immediately responds. Our friend on the other end of the phone laughs and laughs with joy!

It's hard to say good-bye to this little fellow, but we know that in order to return to the office, we must retrace our steps when we have seen all the birds in their enclosures. And so, after seeing all the birds, we return to the barred owl and he begins hooting. By this time, we have learned that he is blind. Well, he sure knows how to HOOT even without eyesight!

Yes, there are wonderful birds at Wild Wings. We see a bald eagle, which is not bald. Its head is white because he is at least five years old, we are told. He also has one long white feather. We see a golden eagle, a barn owl, a screech owl, etc., and we even see a bobcat that has an injury of some type so he cannot remain in the wild. We see him walking and we do not notice any injury.

When we say good-bye to all the birds and the bobcat, we return to the office where the man behind the main desk begins telling us about transporting birds to schools for the children to view. He says he particularly shows birds to inner city school children who are fed breakfast and lunch daily because there is not enough food at their homes. He knows these children would never have an opportunity to see birds of prey.

Yes, Margaret and I have a wonderful time today with the birds, and next Thursday we expect to speak about them on television. Maybe the barred owl will find a way to join us and send hoots!

From Margaret:

Several years ago when we visit a bird sanctuary, we meet Ron Walker, a well-known speaker on birds of prey. I remember the two little Screech-Owls he shows us, one grey and one orange-red, who love him. We want to see him and his birds again. But now we learn that he has retired and some of his birds are in Wild Wings.

Barbara and I decide to visit Wild Wings and we dress warmly because it is a cold day, just above freezing temperatures. We need to be prepared for exhibits that are outside.

I can't wait to reach Wild Wings. I have a life-long connection to birds and I love watching hawks and eagles fly. Also, I love songbirds and bright colored birds of spring and summer. When we reach Wild Wings, a volunteer staff member shows us Screech-Owls that have either gray or reddish-brown feathers for camouflage. The color depends on where they live. The gray Screech-Owl is from the northern part of the country where there are large, gnarly gray oak trees. Hence, the gray Screech-Owls blend in perfectly. The red-brown Screech-Owl comes from the southern part of the country where the trees are more reddish in color, so they fit in perfectly. This is a delight for me to learn.

The next bird fact I learn is that when the Barn Owl flies, it is totally silent. Not a sound is heard and so they can come upon their prey without sound. Later, I check on the Internet why there is no sound and I find that the wing feathers have serrated edges like little combs. These break up the air and so the air moves over the wings almost soundlessly. Any noise is absorbed by the soft down feathers on the wings and legs. No one can hear the approach of an owl.

Also on the Internet, I see a wonderful video by BBC comparing the flight sound of a pigeon, a hawk and an owl. The owl wins by being the most silent.

When we are at Wild Wings, we have an amazing surprise when we greet a seated Barred Owl who is facing Barbara. He begins hooting her. We phone our friend SilverStar, a Native American, to share with her the wonderful sound of the Barred Owl.

Later, when we return to greet the Barred Owl again, this time he is sitting with his back to us. But when we approach, he turns his head completely around so his head looks like it was over his back. Wow. How is this possible?

We now learn that the Barred Owl can rotate his head 270 degrees in each direction because the neck is constructed with two arteries. These arteries connect in the front and back of the owl's brain so the blood supply is not cut off with all the twisting and turning of the head.

In another enclosure we see a Northern Goshawk flying from branch to branch to our delight. I notice that the underbody of the hawk is light in color and the back and head are dark. In flight, the hawk would not be visible when viewed from below. Because he flies on a level with us, we can enjoy this understanding of camouflage.

As we walk past the Great Horned Owl, a male, he sits quietly watching us. It looks like he has two large horns or ears on the top sides of his head. Later on the Internet, I learn that the tuff-like feathers help identify the owl for his family in dense woodlands. Also, they can appear to be bigger to a potential threat and their coloring can also blend into a branch or tree trunk. They are solid in their presence and a delight to observe close up or at a distance.

At Wild Wings we speak with John Ninfo, a volunteer interpreter guide who delights us with many facts about the birds. This inspires me later to search more on the Internet. John Ninfo also sponsors outreach education programs about the birds of prey for the inner city schools whose students might not travel to Wild Wings where they can see and learn about the birds at first hand. He gives us an important notice about the grand opening tomorrow of the new Seneca Art and Culture Center at Ganondagan. We will be there and we will write about this visit in our next chapter.

———————————————————————

CHAPTER 10

NATIVE AMERICAN GANONDAGAN

J oint Journals:

First from Barbara:

Ganondagan is the site of the only still functioning ancient Native American Seneca town in the United States. Margaret and I stand with others outside a newly built center here. It is October 24, the opening of the Seneca Art and Culture Center, and we are ready to observe the opening ceremony. Several men are wearing traditional Seneca regalia, and the director of the opening is one of them. He speaks in both Seneca and English languages, and he explains that this opening ceremony is based on Peace because Ganondagan is a Town of Peace, and all who visit are treated in a peaceful manner.

The new center will present the ancient history of the Senecas and will show that today their language is still maintained as well as their custom of living the same as during ancient times. When the opening ceremony is complete, we file into the new building to sit in the auditorium to watch traditional dancing and singing and to listen to story telling. The young and the old participate, many wearing traditional dress.

Then we visit a large exhibition room to view many, many Seneca artifacts that have survived over the years. Of particular interest to me at the Seneca Art and Culture Center is learning about white corn, one of three vital foods eaten. The other two are beans and squash. 1,400 years ago is not an exaggeration of when corn began growing at Ganondagan, and it fed many people. Then, during a dispute concerning fur trade with early French settlers, the corn was completely destroyed. 500,000 bushels, we are told.

However, seed-savers maintained the seed and today efforts are being made to push forward white corn with the thought that extensive corn production can happen again. It is believed that this healthy food will have healthy benefits for those eating it.

The center has a shop where one can buy white corn and recipes. Before leaving, we have forgotten to enter this shop! Mistake! We want to buy white corn.

We will return! Soon.

From Margaret:

For the October 24 opening of the Seneca Art & Culture Center at Ganondagan, we arrive early to avoid parking worries. Gulf carts are ready to take us to the front of the new center for the opening ceremony.

We stand outside the newly built center with others waiting for this important event. At 10 sharp, G. Peter Jemison, Ganondagan State Historic Site Manager, welcomes everyone to the Culture Center. He says the Seneca people lived at the edge of the forest and welcomed visitors who had come a long way. The pathway, he explains, had many thorns, burs, and thistles, and in the old days, these were removed from their garments when the visitors were welcomed. A fine doeskin cloth was given to them to wipe their eyes if clouded with grief. Then the visitors could see clearly the beauty of the surroundings. Their ears were wiped so they could hear beautiful speaking. Fresh water was given to clear their throats so talking could be shared without hindrance.

While Jemison is speaking, the nearby water fountain turns on and starts running where we are standing. A photographer with his camera is nearby. Maybe he hit it unknowingly. Maybe the Water Spirits want their presence known. In any case, I feel this is a blessing. The Nature Spirit Guardians are here.

Now the visitors are invited inside and we enter. There is a feeling of great joy in seeing this building accomplished with well-designed exhibits. The collections are accessible and framed by a broad expanse of windows that bring inside the beautiful view of Nature. I am pleased. When we enter the exhibition area, we immediately go to the image of the Peace Tree where the Peacemaker urged that weapons be buried under the tree so there would be peace among the people. This is a major symbol for the people and it happened many years ago.

I am especially interested in the beaded belt exhibit because history is woven into the belt. There is the Two Row belt and the Iroquois League belt and now there is a new belt representing native and non-native people united and coming together at the Cultural Center. This new belt was presented at the opening of the Seneca Art and Culture Center.

In the big auditorium, we attend a vibrant social dancing performance with singing and drumming. The dancing is complex with high energy and precise footwork. Men, women and young people dance together or separately in a beautiful, coordinated way that is both joyful and serious. Wow. All are strong dancers from the youngest to the oldest. Our hearts sing, rejoicing.

We then listen to storytelling and we watch the film of the Iroquois Creation Story. We love sharing this enjoyment with all the people witnessing the opening events.

From Barbara:

It is now November 18 and we have returned to the center not only to buy the corn we forgot earlier but to recognize the date, November 18, which some Native Americans believe is the date when their ancestors first came to settle on Mother Earth from the constellation Pleiades. Specifically, many of the Cherokee Nation and Lakota Nation are believers. At this time of year, if the sky is clear at night and you are in the Northern Hemisphere, you should be able to look up to see the distinctive cluster of the Pleiades constellation. And, by the way, the original settlers living on the islands of Hawaii also say their homeland was the Pleiades.

As for the Seneca Nation, we do not know if they think their homeland is the Pleiades, and so we do not say Happy Birthday to them.

Here is an interesting aside. When we were at the opening ceremony, we watched a dramatic movie showing a woman being pushed from her homeland somewhere in the sky and landing on a turtle which became Mother Earth. For us, this tends to confirm what we have just written.

And so, November 18, Margaret and I are again at the Seneca Center, and I am thinking about the Peacemaker who appeared during a time of great strife among Native Americans. He went from tribe to tribe to convince the people to be peaceful. When they began agreeing with him, he suggested that their weapons of war be planted beneath a big tree. Even today, a ceremony commemorates this event and a few years ago we attended a ceremony.

In time, a partnership called the Iroquois Confederacy was constructed and the tribes, often called nations, followed peaceful rules.

After White Men were settled in North American, they wanted to live as an independent nation. The rules of the Iroquois Confederacy were examined by head composers wanting a constitution, such as Benjamin Franklin and Thomas Jefferson. Even the first President, George Washington, knew of the Iroquois Confederacy.

I do not know how many ideas stemming from the Iroquois Confederacy were put into the United States Constitution, but here is an interesting fact. At the Capitol building in Washington DC, is a statue of a goddess called Liberty. On her head is an eagle and feathers typical of what is found on honored Native American headdresses.

From Margaret:

Thanksgiving, November 26, is today, and we are no longer at Ganondagan, but I am speaking on television. I am continuing to think about efforts made by Native Americans to have peace between all people, and I am especially interested in ancient origins. Specifically, I am thinking about my encounter with an ancient guardian of the earth whom I saw in a museum. A Native American told me about him and I went to see him. I knew this ancient one was a part of the Native American cultural tradition, unlike mine, and yet I felt this entity was an earth guardian deeply connected to Mother Earth. Afterward I wanted to connect to him in meditation to learn about the times of his origins, but I worried I would not be able to do this.

He answers: You must go back to your origins to meet me at my origins. There is no communication with you seeking outwards, looking at me. Everything has origins within – the stars, the moon, the sun, the trees, the dancing ones.

Respect. Silence. Patience.

Sit with that.

Tap into your dear planet, Mother Earth, and address her origins, her vast power, her creation of all life forms over millennia.

I attend the process. I nurture and give life. I am much too complex and vast to put into verbal communications.

Just sit with the wonder of it all. Take in the sunrise, the sunset, the everything at the same time and rest in zero.

I am there at the beginning and have traveled to the now and will accompany the Earth going forward. Perhaps we will meet again... and again... and.......

The reply of this ancient one touched me and it prompted me to think about Mother Earth and her origins. She hears my thoughts and responds:

My origins are in my central core so very deep into my center. I am made up of all the elements of the universe, put together, grown in beauty and in power. Many environments are on my surface from white crystalline beaches to volcanic black boulders. Cold, hot, freezing, snow, storms, soft breezes. Every condition. Every delight.

Layers and layers of rocks are my letters and my histories. I am a library of possibilities, pages and pages of scenarios, from the largest to the smallest. Follow one thought line and see where it ends. I provide all this for my inhabitants.

Be gracious. Be humble. Be grateful for the ride.

If humanity could stop for five minutes at noon and breathe the air and SEND AND BE LOVE, then there would be peace on Earth.

From your Mother Earth

I reply to her, Happy Thanksgiving, dear Mother Earth.

From Barbara:

November 26, Thanksgiving Day television talk.

Every year North Americans celebrate Thanksgivings on the fourth Thursday of November. Some people call today turkey day because most of us eat turkey. However, one turkey will not be eaten. Every year the President of the United States spares one turkey for its lifetime. But, this year the President spared two.

The first Thanksgiving was in 1621. A ship called the Mayflower had sailed from England to America with everyone on this boat desiring to set up a new home in America. They were headed toward an already established colony but for some reason they missed the proper route to reach this colony and they stopped at a place further north. Eventually, they moved their ship to a place that satisfied them for starting a settlement.

Two Native American men came up to them speaking excellent English. This was a surprise and then they learned that one of the Native Americans had been kidnapped and taken to England. These two Native Americans and their tribe helped make a new settlement for the newcomers.

Their first corn harvest was successful and the newcomers decided to celebrate their good fortune by having a feast. They invited the local Native Americans to come and many came. The celebration lasted three days and the atmosphere was joyful.

To end this, I want to say that most people think that the Native Americans and newly arrived settlers were not friendly, but the year 1621 and the first Thanksgiving showed that there was good feeling between the new arrivals and the Native Americans.

From Margaret:

I have a special interest in Native American beaded belts and I have been investigating them. Here is what I have learned.

They are called Wampum and they are made mostly from white and purple mollusk shells. These belts hold the histories and treaties of Native Americans in the northern area of the United States.

Barbara has spoken about the treaty called Iroquois Confederacy of this region. The symbol of the Iroquois Confederacy is the Hiawatha Belt that records the five original nations of the Confederacy. These nations agreed to live together in peace. On the Hiawatha Belt, the center tree represents the Onondaga nation where the Peacemaker planted the Tree of Peace. Under this tree the leaders buried their weapons of war. And then they held council. On either side of the tree (Onondaga nation) are squares representing the other four original nations - Seneca, Cayuga, Oneida, and Mohawk. The lines between them show friendship and peace.

As an aside, I have checked the Internet for a picture of the new Wampum belt presented at the Seneca Art and Culture Center opening. I have found a small one being held at the opening presentation.

One year Barbara and I attended a commemoration of the planting of the Peace Tree which initiated peace for the nations here. When we were there, a peace pole was planted. Today there are 200,000 plus peace poles planted throughout the world -- all with the energy of peace.

And so, now there is the coming together of two strong energies, the Tree of Peace and the Peace Pole.

Let us all think peace. Be peaceful.

Mother Earth has said: *If humanity could stop for five minutes at noon and breathe the air and SEND AND BE LOVE, then there would be peace on Earth.*

CHAPTER 11

TO MOTHER EARTH, WITH LOVE

Joint Journals:

First from Barbara:

We have learned from James Tyberonn that our planet and everything on it will be faced with intense energy which has been preplanned for a very long time. He has sent channeling from Archangel Metatron that changes are happening throughout the cosmos, not just the Earth, and so we can understand that it will be an intense moment. Our planet, as we are told, is ascending. What does this mean? We will be able to expand our three-dimensional minds so that we will be in contact with higher intelligences in our cosmos.

I have sent this message to the Global Meditations Network:

November 11 through 25 is a period of planetary configurations that can be a challenge and so it is suggested that you hold a peaceful mind, a calm mind for the next two weeks, sending out thoughts of love. What you think must be counted.

Also, during this two-week time period, meteors are coming in with intense energy. You can change that energy into love.

From Margaret:

I would like to tell you about shared thoughts with Saint Germain.

Meteor showers, lights from the constellation Taurus, are now coming to earth. More will come later this month and some will come in December.

Earth receives the meteor lights and accepts. Humanity can accept the lights and particles of the meteors as a gift, and then can balance them and send them on in peace and harmony.

For this work, what is needed is that humanity goes beyond the self by diminishing selfishness and self-centeredness, and by expanding to the whole earth frequency, the planetary frequency, and universal frequencies. Humanity needs to open its eyes, ears, and heart to expand.

Everyone works at his or her own frequency, resonance, and harmony to balance and expand the light quota. Reaching higher dimensions is obtained by using the dial tone called frequency.

Humans can connect to what is beyond this planet. Meteor showers allow one to reach a higher level of operation. Joy, expansion of mind, heart, and spirit is the result.

What is wanted is Balance, Peace, Love and Light.

[The above shared thoughts with Saint Germain are given to the world on November 5 by Brazil PAX TV.]

Also from Margaret:

It is early morning and I thank Mother Earth for the ride, for the ride of my life at this time. I feel the presence of the angels. I float on the music, Musical Rapture, the music of the angels. When the angelic choir comes in, I feel enveloped by their love. I am wrapped in their blanket of love. I see, feel, that the angels so want to affect the life forms on earth, especially humans, sending them, blanketing them with love, the highest frequency.

I feel Mother Earth is surrounded by their positive energy, the frequency of love – pure love – love that wishes the best for everyone – love that heals, love that brings and gives Joy. They only want the best for Mother Earth, and that all live in Peace.

I fall asleep and dream of Love. Love is the beginning and the end.

OM.

*See Glossary: Musical Rapture.

———————————

From Barbara:

As it turns out, the meteors come a bit early. Via the computer, we see a meteor streaking into Hungary. When a meteor streaks into Bangkok, Thailand, this is well advertised. How many more are coming? Probably a lot more.

We are told by James Tyberonn that these meteors have codings for our earth. Good codings to help the Ascension. I want to mention again here that we can expect disruptions and we should float along without disturbed minds until these disruptions are gone.

———————————

From Margaret:

Crystals can help during this intense time. To help me, I am wearing Lapis Lazuli for the soul, Malachite for strength and Rose Quartz for joy. Edgar Cayce spoke about Lapis Lazuli for soul development, psychic development, and also it is known for healing. Everyone has to make up his or her own mind about crystals.

I have received this channeling from the crystals:

Choose the crystals you are most compatible with. Decide how you wish to interact with them. Crystals can set a balance tone in your environment, giving radiance to the eye and to the heart.

Crystals are healers, lifters of mood, strengtheners of mood, bringers of joy. Crystals are constant. They do not go up and down with emotions. They shine light.

Crystals are full of energy – positive energy. Match your energy to theirs and be uplifted.

It is never a cloudy day when the crystals are present. Crystals light up the environment and transmit Love, Light and Peace.

Crystals are here to serve the planet.

With love from the Crystals.

From Barbara:

We are beginning to realize that a number of explosions in the form of earthquakes are happening along the Ring of Fire which is the Pacific Ocean. We perceive that this intense energy is being helped by the meteors and we think Mother Earth needs help. Thoughts must be counted. Many creating positive thoughts of action can help. I am sending the following message to the Global Meditations Network:

At this moment, the Ring of Fire needs help. This is the Pacific Ocean and surrounding lands. Mother Earth is removing pressure within her by exhaling much energy in the form of earthquakes and volcanic eruptions. The Internet will show you there are tremendous explosions in South America, and there are continual eruptions in Alaska, Japan, etc.

With your mind, you can help by visualizing calm.

I suggest you print out a Ring of Fire (Pacific) picture and overlay it with Dr. Emoto's perfect water crystal, which you will find on his website. On his website, you will also find an explanation of the consciousness of water.

*See Glossary: Dr. Emoto perfect crystal and consciousness of water.

I suggest you play Patricia Cota-Robles' Music Rapture while you are helping the Ring of Fire. You can freely download her music.

*See Glossary: Musical Rapture.

This email is being sent world wide. Remember, common thoughts have much energy. Let us join to help bring Peace, Love and Light to the Ring of Fire.

As for Margaret and me, we are using a 15-inch Stargate to help Mother Earth reduce the tension within the Ring of Fire.

Within the Stargate, we place three important items. A map of the Ring of Fire. A picture of Dr Emoto's exquisite complex water molecule to help the entire Pacific. The third item is a picture of Aborigines playing their didgeridoos which has often helped us to reduce pressure on the Pacific plate. Also, because Pele is the head one for the Pacific, we want to speak with her about what we are doing for the Ring of Fire.

Barbara Wolf & Margaret Anderson

Pele channels to me (Barbara):

You have been cruising along on an even keel all day. The Ring of Fire is an entity, a conscious entity. You have been conceiving of the whole, not one place that has destruction, another place that may be injured, etc.

You have conceived of the Ring of Fire as one conscious entity living on Mother Earth. Your thoughts have been pure all day.

Thank you. Your consciousness helps us to improve. Those around the world who are following your example are helpful, too.

Pele

From Margaret:

Dear Pele, we are trying hard to stabilize the Ring of Fire from the disruptions of earthquakes and volcanoes. We were aiming for balance and harmony. We want peace on the land and within the people – peace reflected in the perfect water crystal of love, divine love of prayer.

Pele, Goddess of Fire, we give you our thoughts and ask for your comment.

Pele answers: Margaret, the last time we were together in meditation I showed you the rainbow. One was starting to occur today. You noticed the beginning.

Fire is the key to plate expansion and movement. Agitation within the humans and off-world gifts of meteors can disrupt the surface calm. Volcanoes need to release the pressure buildup. Earthquakes are the result of earth movement.

When humanity works for Mother Earth's stability with Love, honor and respect, then I am pleased. The animals, birds, deer, dolphins, whales do this naturally. The flowers hold the love frequency. The crystals, the shells, designs of Nature, are in perfect harmony. It is good that humans are coming on board.

The Fire is always present. I am always here.

Pele

From Barbara:

November 13, Paris, France, there is an unexpected attack at a concert packed with people. Terrorists burst in and start shooting with automatic weapons, killing and wounding many. At the same time, in a packed sports stadium, two explosives are detonated and hundreds are startled. Immediately, France goes into high alert as well as other European nations.

November 14, I send out this message to the Global Meditations Network.

The computer brings us together. You can live next door to me or across the world and the computer will bring us together immediately.

Last night there was an unexpected big disturbance in Paris. Many killings, many receiving Post Traumatic Stress Disorder, an imbalance. The computer immediately spreads this imbalance. We need the world to return to balance and thoughts of Peace, Love and Light energies. Please help.

Investigators say a mountain in India called Arunachala has such strong balance, it is the only place on the planet that never shifts. Perhaps you will want to print out a picture of balanced Arunachala and put this energy with your thoughts of Peace, Love and Light energy for the world.

Here is more information on Arunachala. The Hindus believe this mountain is Shiva who represents God. Every year a big fire is built at the top of the mountain to acknowledge Shiva and God. This fire helps to bring purity and truth, and it helps to destroy evil. It is my understanding that the Hindus also believe the ego needs to be cleaned of negativity, and this mountain, Arunachala, will help.

I want to tell you that our friend Carmen Balhestero was sent to Arunachala by Saint Germain who probably knew beforehand what would be happening in Paris before it happened. He wanted her to be at the most balanced place in the world.

We talk to Carmen by SKYPE, and we also print out a photograph of this most balanced place in the world so we ourselves could use it to help bring balance to the world.

It is interesting, and I do not think it is a coincidence that just now, when there are serious problems on the earth, world healer Braco is giving on the computer free programs of his gazing to soothe the people living on Mother Earth. His gazing has healed hundreds. The computer shows us the number watching the free programs. As an example, it says 5,000 participants from 80 countries. We realize that 5,000 can mean 5,000 computers and maybe 100 are watching from one computer. Who knows how many are actually participating in this healing event! Again, thoughts must be counted. Thousands of positive thoughts can weaken the negative. Thousands unified by watching the peace energy of Braco can counter Mother Earth's stomachaches of earthquakes as well as human negative energies that have shaken Paris.

*See Glossary: Braco.

Here is channeling concerning Braco received by Margaret through Saint Germain.

Braco these days is sending out the frequency of love and healing – the world is unified by the focus on his peace and Light. There is a unified field of consciousness which links the entire world. Each person is directed, is focused on Braco, and love and healing is radiated outwards. In this exchange, the frequency of the humans on Earth rises.

We speak this day as a witness. It is like a sunflower growing and then announcing the growth from the sun which establishes a unified field of Love and growth. All positive energy which is so needed.

From Barbara:

While we are helping to stabilize the Ring of Fire, sad news comes from Switzerland that our dear friend Eric Salvisberg has suddenly died. He was the one who told us less than a year ago that the Pleiadians, considered relatives of native Hawaiians, were ready to establish a sanctuary on the Big Island of Hawaii. A ceremony commemorating this intention was in the process of happening when a volcano suddenly erupted in the area. Eric was keeping us informed.

Even though we learn that Eric is no longer on the planet, Margaret asks him if he can help stabilize the Ring of Fire. We know he has a strong affinity for using crystals for healing and balance.

From Margaret:

Eric, are you helping to stabilize the Ring of Fire?

Eric responds: Yes, I am a part of this, in frequency, working to stabilize the frequencies of the Earth energy lines. Crystals help balance these energies as dolphins and whales help stabilize the water and the air.

I have a deep affinity with the crystals and that is why it is such a joy to work with them. My work continues in this line and beyond.

Your white quartz crystal I gave to you holds my presence and connection. The crystal came to you to be a part of this work. That crystal went all over the world with the others.

The Dolphin Love Frequency is powerful. The crystals enhance it. It is like the songs held in the memories of the crystals. They are the Song Lines that hold the world together. Memories. Past, Present & Future. All is present now to open up and to be read.

With love to you and dear Barbara....

From Eric, your friend just over the next hill.

Barbara comments:

My understanding is that Eric is related to the Cosmic System that is functioning for humanity. In the third dimension, picture that we are living in a house, a box, with no windows. No way to see outside the box. We know there is activity, life, outside the box but we cannot see it. Then one day the door is open and we can recognize vast activity.

Eric was beginning to put his finger on cosmic energy before he physically left us. Now, he is not living in a box without windows. He is living outside the box with many others participating in stabilizing the frequency of Mother Earth.

Again, thoughts must be counted. Thousands of positive thoughts can weaken the negative and counter Mother Earth's stomachaches of earthquakes of negative energies that shake her.

Dear Reader,

We will stop now and send this manuscript to the publisher. Then we will begin writing the next book. Love to all of you, Barbara and Margaret.

GLOSSARY

CHAPTER 2: SEDONA
Lynman Whitaker, wind sculptor: http://www.whitakerstudio.com

Bearcloud, artist: http://www.bearcloudgallery.com

The Stargate Experience: http://www.thestargateexperience.com

---

CHAPTER 3: SEDONA
Vortex Symbols and EarthStar Calendar are presented on several pages at end of Glossary.

The Stargate Experience: http://www.thestargateexperience.com

---

CHAPTER 4: MOUNT SHASTA
Carmen Balhestero: http://dopranaaluz.blogspot.com

Telos books, Mount Shasta Light Publishing:
http://www.mslpublishing.com

CHAPTER 5: MOUNT SHASTA
More on Telos:
http://www.mslpublishing.com/pages/Adama%27s-Corner.html

Shasta music: http://www.shastasong.com

PAX TV: http://paxtv.com.br

CHAPTER 6: NIAGARA FALLS
Tesla: https://en.wikipedia.org/wiki/Nikola_Tesla

CHAPTER 7: NIAGARA FALLS
Vortex Symbols: See several pages at end of Glossary.

CHAPTER 8: POPE FRANCIS COMES TO U.S.A.
Emma Kunz, healer: http://www.emma-kunz.com/english/

CHAPTER 11: TO MOTHER EARTH, WITH LOVE
Musical Rapture: http://www.eraofpeace.org/musical-rapture-mp3

Dr. Emoto perfect crystal:
http://fractal.fractalenlighten.netdna-cdn.com/wp-content/
uploads/2012/11/water-molecule-structure-after-the-prayer-at-
Fujiwara-dam.jpg

Dr. Emoto consciousness of water:
http://fractalenlightenment.com/14121/spirituality/
dr-masaru-emoto-on-human-consciousness-and-water

Braco world healer: http://www.braco.me/en/

Vortex Symbols And Earthstar Calendar

Chief Golden Light Eagle and Grandmother SilverStar have given us valuable information on how to use powerful energy fields to help Mother Earth and all that live on her. This information has come from sacred ceremony and the information is available through:

1. Maka Wicahpi Wicohan: Universal and Spiritual Laws of Creator, Star Law Manual of the Galactic Federation. Copyright 1996 by Standing Elk. New Title: The Symbols. The Universal Symbols and Laws of Creation: *A Divine Plan by Which One Can Live*, The Heavenly Hosts, The Servants of Creator.

2. The Vortexes, The Universal Symbols and Laws of Creation: *A Divine Plan by Which One Can Live*, The Heavenly Hosts, The Servants of Creator. Copyright 2013 Revised Edition. All Rights Reserved.

3. The EarthStar Way Calendar, A Sacred Cosmic Earth Moon Sun MorningStar Dance with The Seven Stars. The Universal Symbols and Laws of Creation in Day By Day Living. Copyright 1999-2016. All Rights Reserved.

---

http://www.starelders.net and http://www.starknowledgeenterprises.com/the-symbols/#

VORTEX LISTING

Two Star Law Symbols combined make one Vortex.

The **Vortex of Light, Sound and Vibration** is formed by joining the Symbol of the *Universal Law of Light, Sound and Vibration* with the Symbol of *Spiritual Law of Intuition*.

The **Vortex of Integrity** is formed by the *Universal Law of Free Will* combining with the *Spiritual Freedom of Man*. This is a free will planet and can only operate fully when there is complete spiritual freedom of man. There should be freedom with truth and honesty.

The **Vortex of Symmetry** is formed by combining the *Universal Law of Symmetry* with the *Spiritual Law of Equality*. Symmetry means balance between all things, both spiritual and material. As above, so below. Also, equality between male/female, left/right brain, etc.

The **Vortex of Strength, Health and Happiness** is formed with the combining of the *Universal Law of Movement and Balance* with the *Spiritual Strength, Health and Happiness*. In life one has to be balanced to move forward and also one has to move forward to be balanced. Balance is symmetry in motion. With movement and balance come strength and health and happiness.

The **Vortex of Right Relationship** is produced by combining the *Universal Law of Innocence, Truth and Family* with *Spiritual Protection of Family*. This is also a powerful Vortex of social relationship (based on truth) when the concept has moved from the individual to the group.

The **Vortex of Growth** is formed when the *Universal Law of Change* is combined with the *Spiritual Growth of Man*. Change is a basic tenant of life. With spiritual growth, all things thrive. All things change. Nothing is static. Therefore, both the individual and society need the spiritual growth of man. When humanity grows spiritually, then the Vortex of Growth flourishes. In the natural state, all things grow unhindered. With spiritual growth all things thrive.

The **Vortex of True Judgment** is formed by combining the *Universal Law of Judgment* with the *Spiritual Law of Karma*. All actions should be looked at through the eyes of the *Universal Law of Judgment* so that no harm is done and there is no karma. The latter, the consequences of action, can be turned into dharma, teaching. This law applies socially as well as environmentally.

The **Vortex of Perception** is formed by the combining of the *Universal Law of Perception* combined with the *Spiritual Law of Future Sight*. It is important to perceive the impact of one's actions and to use the gift of future sight. Needed now are planetary actions that affect in a good way the lives of the people in relationship to the air, the water, the land, the life on this planet.

The **Vortex of Connection to Life** is formed with the combining of the *Universal Law of Life* with the *Spiritual Law of Choice*. Life is enhanced by correct choices. It is diminished by poor choices. Therefore, choose wisely. Choice and Life are integrally connected.

The **Vortex of True Nature** is formed by the combining of the *Universal Law of Nature* with the *Spiritual Law of Protection*. Nature exists and thrives. It is up to mankind to protect Nature so that all life thrives on this planet.

The **Vortex of Love** is formed by combining the *Universal Law of Love* with the *Spiritual Law of Healing*. One has to have Love to give healing and to receive healing. Love is the greatest healer. People, Nature, all creatures, plants, cells, molecules, atoms, adamantine particles respond to Love. All have a consciousness. Love creates. Love heals. Love is the highest power of all.

A Vortex is formed at the center of a circle of all Vortexes displayed together. This Vortex is called **Universal Unity and Spiritual Integrity**. All Vortexes bring unity. All Vortexes thrive with integrity. Integrity is the foundation of the Vortexes.

Printed in the United States
By Bookmasters